COOKING
for Two

COOKING
for Two

**Comfort Food Recipes for
Couples, Roommates, or Friends**

MARIE W. LAWRENCE

Skyhorse Publishing

Skyhorse Publishing books may be purchased in bulk at special discounts for
sales promotion, corporate gifts, fund-raising, or educational purposes. Special
editions can also be created to specifications. For details, contact the Special Sales
Department, Skyhorse Publishing, 307 West 36th Street, 11th Floor, New York,
NY 10018 or info@skyhorsepublishing.com.

Skyhorse® and Skyhorse Publishing® are registered trademarks of Skyhorse
Publishing, Inc.®, a Delaware corporation.

Visit our website at www.skyhorsepublishing.com.

10 9 8 7 6 5 4 3 2 1

Library of Congress Cataloging-in-Publication Data is available on file.

Cover design by Daniel Brount
Cover image by Bonnie Matthews

Print ISBN: 978-1-5107-5118-7
Ebook ISBN: 978-1-5107-5119-4

Printed in China

*This book is dedicated to my husband,
Bruce, for whom I creatively cook.*

CONTENTS

WELCOME TO *COOKING FOR TWO*

Not so many years ago, many of us lived as part of large and extended households. Much of the food eaten in those households was cooked in large quantities from recipes meant to feed a crowd. My, how times have changed. In a world of single professionals, single parent families, and couples who remain childless by choice, many of the multiple serving cookbooks we grew up with simply don't meet our needs anymore.

A similar quandary befell my husband Bruce and me. Once our kids were all grown, with families of their own, we were left, still appreciative of the family style cooking we enjoyed for years, but not always sure what to do with such large quantities of food.

Thus began the series of recipe transformations that have led to *Cooking for Two*. This isn't a book about using mixes or ordering takeout; it's about ways to create delicious, from-scratch cooking in your home kitchen, whether that kitchen happens to be deluxe and fully equipped, or much more modest.

WHAT ABOUT THOSE CALORIE COUNTS?

First, let me make clear that I am not a nutritionist; I am simply a person who is very interested in nutrition and has chosen to educate myself as much as possible on the subject. Although caloric content is only a small part of the nutritional picture, it is an important one—especially if you are trying to either lose weight or maintain a healthy weight. I have gauged all the calorie counts in this book by using two major sources: reading the labels on the products I use, and Internet research. In the latter instance, I generally visit at least three separate sites to determine the most accurate median count for any particular food; it is amazing how much variation there can be. I then calculate the approximate caloric value of each ingredient I use in any given recipe, depending on the quantity used. One important note: I use only skim milk in my cooking; it will definitely impact the calorie count in certain dishes, and possibly the way they turn out, if you use whole or another higher fat content milk. There are a few smaller ingredients I don't even try to count, such as salt, baking powder, spices, and flavorings such as vanilla. Everything else goes into the calorie-count pool to produce a grand total as well as approximate counts for individual servings. I personally use calorie counts regularly, just to keep tabs on how many I consume in any given day. Knowing approximately how many calories are in a dish is a handy way to satisfy your curiosity about just how much you do eat, and if you're interested in keeping tabs as well, this will make your job a little easier.

DEGREES OF DIFFICULTY

I've included a very subjective guide with each recipe as to how difficult it is to prepare. Because I've been cooking since my age was in the single digits, there's not too much that fazes me anymore, so I sometimes forget what it's like to just be starting out. In general, I've used a combination of a complexity of ingredients, techniques used, and time involved in attempting to determine whether a recipe might be Easy, Moderate, or Complex. In some cases I've even blended two designations into one, just in case I've under or overestimated.

LET'S GET STARTED!

There are five chapters for you to explore, each with different themes and types of recipes. You'll find a blending of them in the final chapter, Festive Feasts. So, just decide where you'd like to begin, and let's get cooking!

BOUNTIFUL BREAKFASTS, BRUNCHES & BAKED GOODS

Trying to bake for two people can be frustrating at times, while buying from the store or bakery can lead to expensive and sometimes less than healthy choices. There are numerous breakfast and bread recipes in this chapter gauged toward smaller households. I think they're actually more fun to bake than many larger-portioned recipes, although there are one or two unique twists to consider.

Perhaps the most challenging aspect of small-batch baking is accurately calculating the correct amount of egg to use. After measuring numerous eggs, I've come up with proportions that work well for each recipe. I choose to utilize fresh eggs in almost all my recipes calling for egg. You can easily store a partial, beaten egg in a small, covered container in your refrigerator for up to three days. You'll find many recipes using small quantities of egg throughout this book, so using it up shouldn't be a problem. Or, you can just add it in to a breakfast egg scramble, if you prefer. In order to measure the egg, first beat it to thoroughly blend the yolk and white but not to make it increase in volume. Measure using either measuring spoons, a medicine dropper, or a mini measure—whatever works best for you. In general, one large egg will yield 3–4 tablespoons of liquid egg.

It's also of note that I use skim milk in all my recipes; if you wish to substitute a different fat content, it may affect how the recipe turns out and/or calorie count.

Aside from your standard measuring and mixing utensils and bowls, recipes in this section may require a 6-cup muffin tin, small baking sheet, individual-sized (4") pie plates, waffle iron, 6" frying pan and/or larger skillet, and a small saucepan.

Recipes here range from egg-based to bread-based and quick breads to yeast rolls and loaves, with sweet and savory variations abounding. There are also a couple of additional breakfast style recipes included in other chapters, including Ham and Egg Pizza (p. 102) and Croque Monsieur or Madame (p. 259).

Peach Parfaits with Crunchy Nut Granola
Moderate

Fresh sweet peaches in season are surely one of life's little luxuries. Although these crunchy and creamy parfaits highlight their flavor perfectly, they're also very tasty when prepared with frozen thawed peaches or with an individual serving of juice-packed peaches.

INGREDIENTS

2 tablespoons orange juice

2 tablespoons honey or maple syrup

2 medium ripe peaches, diced, or 1½ cups frozen peaches, thawed

1 cup plain Greek style yogurt

2 tablespoons ginger mini chips (diced crystalized ginger), optional

1 cup Crunchy Nut Granola

DIRECTIONS

1. Combine the orange juice and honey or maple syrup.

2. Pour the syrup juice mixture over the peaches and allow them to macerate to blend the flavors for at least 5 minutes. Drain this juice from the peaches and mix it with the yogurt, adding in the ginger mini chips at the same time.

3. Layer the granola, yogurt, and peaches twice in two parfait glasses, ending with a final sprinkling of granola. Garnish with a piece of peach in each glass if you wish and enjoy at once.

There are about 480 calories per parfait.

(continued)

Crunchy Nut Granola

This golden, nutty granola is great by itself or topped with fresh berries and milk or half-and-half. In a sealed plastic bag or canister, it will stay fresh for several weeks.

INGREDIENTS

¼ cup packed brown sugar

2 tablespoons corn or canola oil

¼ teaspoon almond extract

2 tablespoons orange juice

⅛ teaspoon salt

1 cup old-fashioned rolled oats

½ cup combination of sliced almonds, chopped pecans

DIRECTIONS

1. Preheat your oven to 350°F.

2. Combine the brown sugar, oil, almond extract, orange juice, and salt, mixing well. Stir in the oats and nuts to coat completely.

3. Spray your baking sheet with non-stick spray, or oil lightly. Pour the granola onto the baking sheet, spreading out well.

4. Bake for 35–40 minutes, stirring occasionally to break up and even browning. Allow to cool completely before placing in an airtight container.

This makes 2 cups of granola; 1110 calories total or 280 per ½ cup serving, 140 per ¼ cup.

Popovers for Two

Easy-Moderate

Have your ingredients at room temperature to facilitate the baking of light and puffy popovers. For an easy shortcut simply place your eggs, still in the shell, in a bowl or cup of hot tap water for about 1 minute to warm it up. This makes six small popovers.

INGREDIENTS

2 large eggs

½ cup milk

½ cup flour

¼ teaspoon salt

3 teaspoons butter

DIRECTIONS

1. Preheat your oven to 400°F.

2. Divide the butter evenly between three muffin cups, staggering the ones used for even baking.

3. Whisk or beat together the eggs and milk. Whisk in the flour and salt until the mixture is smooth but not bubbly; approximately the consistency of heavy cream.

4. Place the muffin tin in the preheated oven for about 1 minute, until the butter melts. Pour the batter evenly into the prepared cups.

5. Bake for 30–35 minutes, until the popovers are deep golden brown and puffed high. Be patient; if you under-bake the popovers, they will deflate once you remove them from the oven.

6. Serve them warm with your favorite jam.

One batch of popovers without condiments equals about 250 to 500 calories , depending on type and amount of jam.

Gougières
Moderate

These cheesy little mounds are basically a savory cream puff without the cream filling. They are delicious for breakfast, brunch, or as an appetizer and are best served hot. The pate a choux mixture may be frozen; drop the batter onto wax paper, sprinkle with the Parmesan cheese, and freeze until firm. Label and store in a sealed zip-lock bag. When ready to bake, place the frozen gougières on your parchment-lined baking sheet and place directly into a preheated oven, allowing just a few more minutes of baking time. This recipe makes 6 little gougières. If you'd prefer them for appetizers, you can form a dozen petite mounds instead, adjusting the baking time down slightly.

INGREDIENTS

¼ cup water

2 tablespoons butter

¼ teaspoon salt

A few grinds black pepper

¼ cup flour

1 egg

¼ cup shredded Gruyère cheese

1 tablespoon grated Parmesan cheese

DIRECTIONS

1. Preheat your oven to 400°F.

2. Place the water, butter, salt, and pepper in a small saucepan. Bring to a full boil over medium high heat.

3. While still boiling, stir in the flour all at once, continuing to cook a minute longer, until the mixture has adhered into a ball.

4. Remove from the heat and beat in the egg until it is smooth and glossy. Set aside for a couple of minutes to just slightly cool; this is a good time to shred the Gruyère cheese.

5. Stir the Gruyère vigorously into the pate a choux mixture and drop in 6 even mounds on a parchment-lined baking sheet.

6. Sprinkle the grated Parmesan evenly over the tops and bake for 25 minutes, until the gougières are puffed and golden. If you wish, pierce the side of each little puff with a sharp knife blade, allowing steam to escape.

7. Serve at once, or if you prefer they may also be enjoyed at room temperature.

*This recipe serves two for breakfast or brunch,
260 calories per serving of three gougières or 520 total.*

Fluffy Waffles for Two
Moderate

Fresh hot waffles, crispy golden on the outside and fluffy light within, put their frozen counterparts to shame. If you have room to tuck away a waffle iron, it's a great investment for many future breakfasts and brunches.

INGREDIENTS

1 egg, separated
½ cup milk
2 tablespoons cooking oil
⅓ cup flour

1 teaspoon baking powder
1 teaspoon sugar
¼ teaspoon salt

DIRECTIONS

1. Preheat your waffle iron and spray with non-stick spray if needed (I prefer to do this even though I have an iron with a non-stick surface).

2. Beat the egg white in a small bowl until it reaches soft peaks; set aside. Combine the egg yolk, milk, and oil in a medium mixing bowl, beating until well combined.

3. Whisk or beat in the combined dry ingredients until the batter is smooth. Gently fold in the beaten egg white until just well combined.

4. Pour about ½ of the batter evenly over the hot iron, cooking until done. Repeat with the rest of the batter.

5. Enjoy hot with butter and maple syrup. For a special treat, top them with fresh berries and whipped cream.

This makes two full-sized waffles at about 295 calories each without toppings.

Gingerbread Waffle with Fresh Orange Butter Sauce

Moderate-Complex

Imagine the sweet, spicy scent of gingerbread wafting from your waffle iron! These waffles are extra rich and delicate, and pair delightfully with Fresh Orange Butter Sauce. Set your waffle iron to a medium low setting so as not to burn your waffle; due to the molasses and sugar content, you don't want it too dark. The trick is to cook it thoroughly enough so that it won't fall apart when you're removing it from the iron, while maintaining the delicate gingerbread flavor. Gently folding the waffle over onto itself while transferring it from the iron to your plate will help in this endeavor; just unfold it as soon as it hits the plate. You can substitute ¼ teaspoon pumpkin pie spice for the mixed spices in the recipe, if you wish.

INGREDIENTS

2 tablespoons butter, melted

1 egg, beaten

⅜ cup sour cream

¼ cup sugar

2 tablespoons molasses

½ cup all-purpose or cake flour

¼ teaspoon ginger

¼ teaspoon cinnamon

¼ teaspoon grated orange zest

¼ teaspoon baking soda

Pinch cloves

Pinch salt

DIRECTIONS

1. Preheat your waffle iron, spraying it with non-stick spray or oiling it lightly.

2. In a small bowl, whisk together the melted butter, egg, sour cream, sugar, and molasses.

3. Whisk in the combined dry ingredients until just well blended.

4. Pour evenly over the hot iron and cook until done. Carefully transfer to your plate and repeat with remaining batter. Top with the warm Fresh Orange Butter Sauce. Feel free to top with an extra dollop of sour cream, if you wish.

This recipe is approximately 470 calories per waffle, before adding sauce or sour cream.

(continued)

Fresh Orange Butter Sauce

2 medium navel oranges, zest grated

2 tablespoons sugar

1 teaspoon cornstarch

1 tablespoon butter

2 teaspoons orange liqueur (optional)

DIRECTIONS

1. Peel and section the orange, saving all the juice.

2. Combine in a small saucepan along with the sugar, cornstarch, and butter. Stir to dissolve the sugar and cornstarch, and then heat to boiling.

3. Remove from heat and stir in the orange liqueur, if desired. Serve warm over your Gingerbread Waffle.

Orange Butter Sauce has about 340 calories total.

Crispy Cornmeal Chicken and Waffles
Complex

The techniques to create this satisfying breakfast or brunch dish are not particularly difficult, but it does require a bit of concentrated attention and timing to have everything ready to eat at the same time. Start by marinating your chicken in the buttermilk mixture; prep the sauce and waffle ingredients while the chicken is tenderizing. Begin frying the chicken just before combining the wet and dry waffle ingredients; if you're really clever you can cook your chicken and waffles simultaneously. Then all you'll need to do is plate, pour on the Cranberry Maple Sauce, and enjoy!

Crispy Chicken

INGREDIENTS

½ cup buttermilk or ½ cup milk mixed with
    1 teaspoon lemon juice

¼ teaspoon salt

Splash Tabasco sauce

2 (4–5-ounce) boneless, skinless chicken
    breasts

2 tablespoons cornmeal

2 tablespoons flour

¼ teaspoon salt or garlic salt

¼ teaspoon paprika

¼ cup corn oil

DIRECTIONS

1. Combine the buttermilk or milk and lemon juice with the salt and Tabasco sauce.

2. Cut each chicken breast into three strips and add them to the liquid, covering all the pieces. Placing it in a zip-lock bag may make this easier to accomplish. Allow it to sit for about 30 minutes; this is a good time to concoct your syrup and get the waffle ingredients assembled.

3. Combine the cornmeal, flour, salt or garlic salt, and paprika and set it aside.

4. Once you're ready to fry the chicken, preheat the oil in a 6" heavy frying pan over medium high heat.

5. Shake the excess buttermilk from the chicken pieces and dredge them evenly in the flour and cornmeal mixture.

6. Quick fry the chicken strips until they are nicely browned on all sides and cooked through; this will only take about 2–3 minutes.

7. Drain on a paper towel while finishing the waffles.

There are approximately 340 calories per serving of chicken.

(continued)

Cornmeal Waffles

INGREDIENTS

2 tablespoons corn oil

1 small egg (about 2 tablespoons)

½ cup buttermilk or ½ cup milk mixed with
   1 teaspoon lemon juice

⅜ cup flour

2 tablespoons cornmeal

1 tablespoon sugar

¼ teaspoon salt

¼ teaspoon baking soda

½ teaspoon baking powder

DIRECTIONS

1. Preheat your waffle iron on a medium high setting; oil or cover the surface with non-stick cooking spray.

2. In a small bowl combine the oil, egg, and buttermilk or milk and lemon juice, whisking to combine well.

3. Stir together the flour, cornmeal, sugar, salt, baking powder, and baking soda in a separate bowl. Just before baking your waffles, add the dry ingredients to the liquid mixture, stirring until just combined.

4. Pour half the batter evenly onto the hot waffle iron and bake until done. Place on your serving plate, and repeat with remaining batter. Top with the fried chicken strips and pour the Cranberry Maple Sauce over all.

One waffle equals about 310 calories before adding chicken and sauce.

(continued)

Cranberry Maple Sauce

INGREDIENTS

1 cup fresh or frozen cranberries

½ cup orange juice

½ cup pure maple syrup

2 tablespoons butter

DIRECTIONS

1. Combine all ingredients in a small saucepan. Bring to a full boil, stirring occasionally.

2. Lower heat and simmer for 2–3 minutes, until the cranberries have softened and burst. You can help this process along if you wish by pressing them with the back of a spoon, or leave a few intact for color and flavor.

3. Serve the syrup warm over the chicken and waffle.

Calories in Cranberry Maple Sauce total approximately 360 per serving.

Pancake Master Mix

Easy

This recipe provides you with 6 mini-batches of pancake mix, ready to combine with a bit of egg, oil, and water whenever you'd like a few pancakes. Leftover pancakes may be stored in plastic wrap or zip-lock bags in the fridge for up to three days, if you have leftovers. Simply pop them in the microwave for a few seconds to reheat. (Hint: I like to butter my pancakes before microwaving; it's easy to apply to the cool pancakes and provides you with a nice gauge of when they're heated through.) Measure out the mix the same as you do the flour, by spooning lightly into the measuring container and leveling off with a straight spoon handle or knife edge.

INGREDIENTS

3¼ cups all-purpose flour

1 cup non-fat dry milk powder

2 tablespoons baking powder

2 tablespoons sugar

1½ teaspoons salt

DIRECTIONS

1. Combine all the ingredients in a large bowl, whisking well so that everything is thoroughly blended.

2. Divide the dry mix evenly between six sandwich-size zip-lock bags; this should equal just about ¾ cup per bag.

3. Label and store in a cool, dry place until you're ready to use. The most perishable item in the mix is the milk powder, so to determine shelf life, check for "use by" date on that package. When you're ready for some pancakes, use the guidelines below.

(continued)

Small Batch Pancakes

INGREDIENTS

¾ cup bag Master Mix

1 tablespoon corn oil

½ cup cold water

½ beaten egg; about 2 tablespoons or 1 egg

DIRECTIONS

1. Whisk all ingredients together until the batter is fairly smooth. Adding a whole egg will give you slightly more crepe-like pancakes; ½ egg will be more like a traditional flapjack. Allow it to rest a minute or two, while your frying pan is getting nice and hot.

2. Check the pan for readiness by sprinkling a few drops of water from your fingertips onto the pan's surface; the water should form little droplets and skitter along the top of the pan.

3. Lightly oil the pan or coat with non-stick cooking spray. Pour the batter in to form 4" diameter pancakes. Cook over medium high heat until the tops form bubbles; carefully flip and fry on the second side until they are evenly golden brown and cooked through.

4. Serve hot with your favorite toppings. This recipe will yield approximately 5–6 pancakes, depending on their size.

Calories per batch (not including frying oil or toppings) are 275 per package of dry mix; about 465 when prepared with ½ egg; about 95 each per 5 pancakes or 75 each per 6 pancakes.

Pumpkin Pancakes

Easy-Moderate

These are a great autumn treat, and also a handy way to utilize small amounts of puréed pumpkin. Other recipes using small quantities of pumpkin purée include Pumpkin Apricot Cheesecake (p. 276) and Curried Pumpkin Apple Soup (p. 280). To save pumpkin for future use, measure out the amount you need for the desired recipes and freeze individually on a wax paper–lined baking sheet. Once they are frozen, seal in a plastic freezer bag, labeled for amount of pumpkin and freezing date. Canned pumpkin purée may be denser than homemade; if necessary, adjust pumpkin and milk ratio to produce a pourable batter. Substitute ¼ teaspoon of pumpkin pie spice for the mixed spices listed if you prefer.

INGREDIENTS

¼ cup milk
¼ cup pumpkin purée
½ egg, beaten: about 2 tablespoons
1 tablespoon butter, melted
1 tablespoon sugar
⅛ teaspoon cinnamon

⅛ teaspoon ginger
⅛ teaspoon salt
Pinch of nutmeg
½ cup all-purpose flour
1 teaspoon baking powder

DIRECTIONS

1. Whisk together the milk, pumpkin purée, egg, melted butter, and sugar until smooth. Add the combined dry ingredients, again whisking smooth.

2. Preheat skillet or frying pan over medium high heat until a drop of water skitters across the surface. Lightly oil the surface and pour half the batter into three equal portions on the hot pan, turning once when the tops form bubbles.

3. Remove to serving plate and repeat with the remaining batter. Serve hot with your choice of toppings.

This equals about 450 calories per batch, not including frying oil or toppings, or about 75 calories for each of 6 pancakes.

Classic French Toast

Easy

Classic French Toast stands quite nicely on its own paired with butter and syrup or jam; add bacon or sausage for even heartier fare. It also forms the basis for other delectable breakfast or brunch dishes such as Caramel Banana French Toast or Berries and Cream French Toast. Baguette style bread is not recommended for this recipe because the slices are not big enough in diameter to absorb the liquid; go for a more rustic type loaf or commercially sliced French or Italian bread. Calories will vary slightly depending on the type of bread used and whether you choose milk or half-and-half for the dipping batter.

INGREDIENTS

2 eggs, beaten

⅜ cup milk or half-and-half

Pinch or 2 of sugar

⅛ teaspoon vanilla extract or a pinch of cinnamon, nutmeg, or cardamom

4 slices French or Italian style bread (not baguette)

2 teaspoons oil or butter

DIRECTIONS

1. In a small bowl, use a fork or small whisk to beat together the egg and milk or half-and-half. Stir in the sugar and desired flavoring.

2. Dip each slice of bread on both sides, allowing it to absorb a goodly amount of the liquid.

3. Heat the butter or oil in a heavy frying pan or skillet over medium heat. Add the dipped slices of bread and allow them to sauté until browned on one side; flip and brown the other side as well.

4. Serve hot with desired toppings.

Made with skim milk and light Italian bread, 2 slices without condiments will be approximately 210 calories; made with half-and-half 255 calories.

Berries and Cream French Toast

Easy

Here's a little bit of sweet indulgence to start your day in style. If you're a coconut lover, you could try substituting Sweet Coconut French Toast (p. 26) in place of the classic listed here.

INGREDIENTS

2 ounces cream cheese

¼ cup heavy cream

2 tablespoons sugar

4–6 drops vanilla, lemon, or orange extract or a small pinch of grated lemon or orange zest

1 recipe Classic French Toast (p. 20) flavored with vanilla extract

2 tablespoons strawberry or raspberry jam

DIRECTIONS

1. In a small mixing bowl, using an electric mixer, beat together the cream cheese, heavy cream, sugar, and flavoring of choice until smooth and creamy; set aside.

2. Prepare the French toast, placing it on the serving plate and spreading it evenly with the jam when done.

3. Mound the whipped cream cheese mixture evenly on each slice and top with berries. Serve at once.

The cream topping and jam are about 300 calories per serving without berries or Classic French Toast. Prepared with strawberries the entire dish will equal about 560 calories per serving; with raspberries 580 calories.

Caramel Banana French Toast

Easy

Slightly under-ripe bananas work best for this recipe. If you wish to be extra indulgent, you can top the whole thing with a dollop of sour cream, whipped cream, or even ice cream, although it's quite tasty all by itself.

INGREDIENTS

2 tablespoons butter

¼ cup packed brown sugar

2 tablespoons orange juice

2 tablespoons half-and-half

½ teaspoon vanilla extract and/or 1 teaspoon rum

1 banana, peeled and thinly sliced

1 recipe Classic French Toast (p. 20) flavored with cinnamon and/or nutmeg or 1 recipe Sweet Coconut French Toast (p. 26)

DIRECTIONS

1. Combine the butter, brown sugar, orange juice, and half-and-half in a small saucepan. Bring to a full boil. Add the vanilla extract or rum.

2. Add the sliced banana and heat for just a few seconds longer to blend flavors without cooking the banana slices. Serve over French toast.

This sauce equals about 270 calories without cream toppings.

Fried Rice Breakfast Patties
Easy

I started concocting this easy-to-cook mixture of rice and egg back when I was in high school, and it remains one of my favorite ways to use up cold cooked rice. This recipe serves two, and is a breeze to make in larger batches. I especially enjoy Fried Rice Breakfast Patties with a side of bacon, although they're also tasty on their own or with a few chopped cashews or peanuts sprinkled over them.

INGREDIENTS

1 cup cooked rice

2 eggs, slightly beaten

1 teaspoon dried onion flakes

1 teaspoon soy sauce

Several grinds of black pepper

2 tablespoons oil

DIRECTIONS

1. Combine the rice, eggs, and seasonings in a small bowl, stirring to combine well.

2. Heat the oil over medium high heat; you want it nice and hot.

3. Spoon half the rice mixture onto the hot oil in three even mounds; it will spread slightly. Cook patties until the edges appear brown, flip and cook on the other side until they are light golden brown on both sides and cooked through; about 2 minutes total. Repeat with remaining rice mixture.

4. Serve hot as is, topped with a little more soy sauce, or with a side of choice.

One serving cooked in corn oil is about 270 calories.

Sweet Coconut French Toast

Moderate

This is a handy way to use up leftover coconut milk and/or sweetened condensed milk. It's rich and sweet enough to enjoy as is, or try topping with jams, fresh berries, or other fruits, or even a drizzle of chocolate sauce for a decadent breakfast treat.

INGREDIENTS

2 tablespoons sweetened condensed milk

⅜ cup coconut milk, regular or light

2 eggs, lightly beaten

4 large slices white bread

4 teaspoons unsalted butter or coconut oil

¼ cup sweetened flaked coconut

DIRECTIONS

1. Beat together the condensed milk, coconut milk, and eggs until smooth; the mixture will be fairly thick and creamy. Allow the bread to soak in the mixture long enough to absorb as much of the liquid as possible.

2. Heat a heavy skillet or frying pan over medium heat. Add the butter or coconut oil, allowing it to melt but not start to brown.

3. Sprinkle the top of each piece of soaked bread with 1½ teaspoons of the coconut, pressing it down lightly. Invert them, coconut side down, into the hot skillet. Sprinkle the rest of the coconut evenly over the remaining sides, again pressing lightly.

4. Sauté the French toast on each side until it is golden brown. Remove from heat and serve at once.

Calories before adding fruit, jam, or syrup are about 510 per serving when prepared with light coconut milk; closer to 580 if using regular coconut milk.

Pie Crust Dough
Moderate

You'll see this pie crust recipe featured in the desserts section of this book as well; it's a versatile recipe that divides easily into portions and freezes well. Simply place in sealable plastic bags or wrap in plastic wrap, label, and refrigerate up to a week or freeze for up to three months.

INGREDIENTS

1 cup all-purpose flour
½ teaspoon sugar
½ teaspoon salt

½ cup butter
½ teaspoon mild vinegar or lemon juice
3 tablespoons cold water

DIRECTIONS

1. Combine the flour, sugar, and salt in a medium-sized mixing bowl.

2. Using a cheese grater, shred the butter into small pieces, or alternatively cut it into the dry ingredients until the mixture resembles coarse crumbs.

3. Combine the vinegar or lemon juice with the water and sprinkle it over the mixture, stirring lightly with a fork until it is all integrated (it may still appear rather crumbly at this point).

4. Gather the dough together with your hands and form into four equal balls. Place in plastic wrap or a plastic storage bag and refrigerate at least half an hour before rolling out for the best results. You may also freeze the dough at this point; when ready to use, remove the amount you need and microwave for just a few seconds at time, until it's thawed enough to roll but still quite cold. Roll out thin on a floured surface and fill your pie plate, leaving a generous overhang for fluting the edges.

There are 1240 calories in the entire recipe; 310 per single crust or 620 when making a double-crusted pie.

Bacon, Broccoli, and Tomato Mini Quiches
Moderate

This tasty breakfast or brunch treat produces two mini quiches. If you've prepared and frozen your pie crust dough in advance, simply remove two portions from the freezer, wrap in plastic or a sandwich bag, and allow them to thaw in the refrigerator overnight. If you're in a hurry the frozen dough may also be cautiously microwaved for just a few seconds, remembering that it should still be quite cold for optimal rolling; try 10–15 seconds to start. You could also prepare and bake the mini quiches in advance if you wish; chill and store in the refrigerator overnight or up to three days. To reheat, place in a preheated 375°F oven for 15–20 minutes.

INGREDIENTS

2 individual portions Pie Crust Dough (p. 27)

⅔ cup chopped broccoli, cooked tender crisp

4 slices bacon, cooked crisp

½ cup cherry tomatoes, halved

½ cup shredded cheddar cheese

1 large egg

¼ teaspoon powdered mustard

⅛ teaspoon onion powder

⅛ teaspoon salt

¼ teaspoon mixed Italian herbs

½ cup evaporated skim milk or ⅓ cup powdered milk mixed with ½ cup water

DIRECTIONS

1.   Preheat oven to 375°F; place rack in middle upper position. Roll each portion of pie crust out and fit loosely into 6" pie pans, making high fluted edges on each.

2.   Divide evenly in order between the two pie pans the cooked broccoli, crumbled bacon, halved cherry tomatoes, and cheddar cheese.

3.   Beat together the egg, powdered mustard, onion powder, salt, and herbs. Stir in the milk until everything is well blended. Pour gently over the bacon, cheese, and vegetables in each pie shell.

4.   Bake for 20–25 minutes, until the filling is somewhat puffed and set. Serve warm or chilled; be sure to refrigerate any leftovers.

This makes two mini quiches for a total of 620 calories for the crust and 555 for the filling; 1175 calories; approximately 590 per single serving.

Ham, Cheese, and Spinach Mini Quiches
Moderate

This pair of savory mini quiches combines classic ham and cheese with a bit of garlic sautéed spinach for extra flavor and nutrition. Enjoy them for breakfast, brunch, lunch, or supper.

INGREDIENTS

3 ounces fresh spinach or ¼ box frozen chopped spinach, thawed

½ small clove garlic, minced or ¹⁄₁₆ teaspoon garlic powder

2 teaspoons olive oil

2 ounces sliced cooked ham, diced

1 large egg

½ cup evaporated skim milk or ⅓ cup powdered nonfat dry milk mixed with ½ cup water

⅛ teaspoon dry mustard

3–4 drops Tabasco or other pepper sauce

Pinch of grated nutmeg

⅛ teaspoon salt

2 individual portions Pie Crust Dough (p. 27)

2 ounces Swiss or Gruyère cheese, shredded (½ cup)

DIRECTIONS

1. Sauté the spinach and garlic in the olive oil until it is wilted but still bright green. Add the diced ham and set aside.

2. Beat together the egg, evaporated milk, dry mustard, Tabasco sauce, nutmeg, and salt until smooth.

3. Roll out the chilled pie crust dough into two rounds large enough to fit in the pie plates with adequate overhang to form fluted edges. Once the pie crusts are completed, divide the spinach/ham mixture evenly between the two pie plates.

4. Sprinkle the cheese on top and pour the egg mixture evenly over all.

5. Bake at 375°F for approximately 30 minutes, until the crust is slightly browned and the filling soft set.

Total calories in this recipe are 1150; 575 for each mini quiche.

Mexicali Omelet

Moderate-Complex

This hearty and flavorful omelet will feed two people with modest appetites. If you're a red bean lover, canned is the easiest and quickest way to go. If you're not sure about using the rest of the can, simply pre-cook 2 tablespoons of dried small red beans according to the package instructions, adjusting the salt in the recipe to your preference.

INGREDIENTS

1–2 teaspoons fresh chopped cilantro

2 teaspoons lime or lemon juice

⅛ teaspoon salt

¼ teaspoon cumin or chili powder, divided

½ tomato, diced

¼ Hass avocado, peeled and diced

2 slices bacon, diced

3 teaspoons oil or bacon fat, divided

¼ cup canned red beans

½ teaspoon instant minced onion

⅛ teaspoon cumin or chili powder

2 eggs

Dash of hot sauce

Pinch of salt

2 teaspoons water

¼ cup shredded Monterey Jack or mild cheddar cheese

A few slices of jalapeño or bell pepper, depending on taste

Sour cream, optional

Ripe olives, optional

Tortilla chips or Honey Cornbread (p. 51) for accompaniment

DIRECTIONS

1. Combine the chopped cilantro, lime or lemon juice, ⅛ teaspoon salt, ⅛ teaspoon cumin or chili powder, and the diced tomato and avocado in a small bowl; set aside.

2. Sauté the diced bacon in a small skillet until it is crispy and golden; drain the bacon fat and measure back in 1 teaspoon or add a teaspoon of oil.

3. Add in the beans, onion, and ⅛ teaspoon cumin or chili powder. Cook, stirring occasionally and mashing the beans down, until the mixture is thick and creamy; check for seasoning, adding a bit of salt and cooking/canning liquid if necessary. Set aside while preparing the omelet.

4. Beat together the eggs, hot sauce, pinch of salt, and water. Heat two teaspoons of the bacon fat or oil in a small skillet over medium high heat. Pour in the egg mixture, tilting the pan and lifting the corners of the omelet as it cooks. If you prefer, simply flip it over midway through the cooking process; just don't overcook.

5. Remove the pan from the heat and place the bean mixture on half the omelet, followed by the cheese and peppers. Fold it in half and slide onto your serving plate.

6. Top with the marinated diced tomatoes and avocado. Serve accompanied by sour cream, olives, and cornbread or tortilla chips, if you wish.

This omelet is 565 calories without added condiments.

Sweet Apple and Brie Omelet
Easy-Moderate

My gluten-free daughter-in-law describes this omelet as tasting somewhat like French toast. It's a nice change from savory egg dishes, whether you enjoy it for breakfast, brunch, or possibly even as a variation on dessert! This makes a light meal for two. If you wish, double the ingredients and then divide mixture in half for cooking.

INGREDIENTS

1 tablespoon raspberry jam

1 tablespoon orange juice

2 eggs

½ teaspoon sugar

Pinch of salt

Pinch of cinnamon

1 tablespoon milk

2 teaspoons butter

1 ounce sliced or diced Brie cheese

Apple slices, unpeeled or peeled as you wish

DIRECTIONS

1. Heat together the jam and orange juice until the jam is melted, stirring to mix well; set aside.

2. Beat the eggs with a fork until the yolks and whites are fully incorporated. Beat in the sugar, salt, cinnamon, and milk.

3. Heat the butter in a small skillet over medium heat until it is frothy but not browned. Gently pour in the eggs, and sauté in the butter, tilting the pan and lifting the edge of the omelet to ensure an even cooking process. If you prefer, simply turn the partially cooked omelet over midway through. In order to ensure a tender omelet, heat only until the egg is just set.

4. Immediately place the Brie on half the omelet and place the apple slices over the Brie. Flip the other half of the omelet over the filled portion and carefully remove to a serving plate. Pour the warm jam sauce over the top and serve.

There are approximately 350 calories total in this omelet (175 calories per serving).

Potallium Frittata
Moderate-Complex

You won't find the word potallium in any dictionary; it's my own descriptive term for the ingredients in this frittata. Besides the requisite eggs and cheese, it includes both potatoes and members of the genus Allium, a.k.a. the family of flowering plants otherwise known as onions, garlic, chives, leeks, scallions, and their various relatives. I suggest using your favorite type of onion or leek as the main component, along with finely minced garlic, and a sprinkling of chives to top it off. If you have other allium, such as scallions or shallots, that you'd like to integrate, feel free! This makes two small-ish servings.

INGREDIENTS

1½ teaspoons butter

1½ teaspoons olive oil

¼ cup thinly sliced onions or leeks

1 medium small red skinned potato, scrubbed and thinly sliced (¾ cup)

½ clove garlic, minced

2 eggs

Salt and pepper or seasoned salt

¼ cup shredded Gruyère cheese

1 tablespoon chopped chives

Sour cream, optional but good

DIRECTIONS

1. Place a 6" skillet over medium heat; add the butter and olive oil, swirling occasionally until the butter melts. Add in the sliced onions or leeks and cook for a minute or two, until they just begin to wilt.

2. Add the potato and minced garlic and continue cooking for about 5 minutes, until the potatoes are crisp, tender, and starting to lightly brown.

3. Meanwhile, beat the eggs with a few shakes of seasoned salt or salt and pepper to taste.

4. Arrange the potato/onion mixture in an even layer, sprinkling them with a little seasoned salt or salt and pepper as well. Carefully pour the eggs evenly over the top and cook until the edges appear done and the middle is mostly set.

5. Sprinkle with the grated Gruyère and finish the cooking process in a 375°F oven, just until the cheese melts; this will probably only take a couple of minutes.

6. Remove from the oven, sprinkle with chives, and cut into wedges to serve with sour cream.

In the whole frittata there are about 470 calories without sour cream; add 50 for every 2 tablespoons you choose to add. Divide in half if shared between two people.

Italian Kitchen Frittata
Moderate

This frittata makes me think of sunny gardens and kitchens fragrant with the scents of summer. Add some crusty bread for a delicious light meal most any time of the day. As with the other frittata and omelet recipes, this will provide a lighter meal for two.

INGREDIENTS

3 teaspoons olive oil, divided
½ cup sliced baby portabella mushrooms
½ cup thinly sliced zucchini
Garlic powder or finely minced garlic
Freshly ground salt and pepper

2 eggs
1 small or ½ medium tomato, thinly sliced
⅛ teaspoon mixed Italian herbs
¼ cup shredded mozzarella or smoked
    provolone/mozzarella blend

DIRECTIONS

1. Heat 2 teaspoons of the olive oil in a small ovenproof skillet over medium high heat. Add the sliced mushrooms and zucchini; sprinkle lightly with garlic or garlic powder and grind some salt and pepper over all. Sauté the vegetables, turning frequently, until they are tender, crisp, and beginning to lightly brown.

2. Meanwhile, beat the eggs until the yolks and whites are thoroughly combined. Add the hot cooked vegetables to the eggs, add the remaining teaspoon of oil to the pan, and quickly pour the eggs and veggies into the hot oil. Cook for 2–3 minutes over medium high heat, until the edges appear set but the middle is still slightly moist.

3. While it is cooking, arrange the tomato slices over the top of the frittata. Sprinkle the slices with a bit of additional garlic powder, grind on some salt and pepper, and sprinkle the Italian herbs over all.

4. Sprinkle the cheese over everything and place the frittata, pan and all, into a preheated 375°F oven. Bake for about 5 minutes, until the cheese has melted. Remove from the oven, cut in slices, and enjoy.

There are about 390 calories in the entire frittata, or 195 in each half.

Ciabatta with Honey Lime Cream Cheese and Mango
Easy

Easy to prepare and delicious, this recipe works equally well with split ciabatta buns or plain bagels. If you're watching calories you may prefer to substitute low-fat cream cheese in place of the regular. Fresh diced peaches may be substituted for the mango if you prefer; in a pinch, even canned will do.

INGREDIENTS

1 medium mango, diced (1 cup)

1 tablespoon lime juice

¼ teaspoon shredded lime zest

2 tablespoons honey

4 ounces cream cheese

2 ciabatta buns or bagels

DIRECTIONS

1. Combine the diced mango with the lime juice, lime zest, and honey. Set it aside to macerate for about 5 minutes to allow juices to form.

2. Mash the cream cheese with a fork to soften it. Stir in about 2 tablespoons of the juice from the mango mixture until the cream cheese is smooth and creamy.

3. Spread the cheese mixture on the split ciabatta buns or bagels. Spoon the fruit over the top, place the other half of the bun on top, and enjoy at once.

The total calories using a ciabatta bun, mango, and regular cream cheese equal 610 per sandwich.

Lemon Ginger Scones
Moderate

Nothing says a relaxing weekend breakfast like freshly baked scones and a steaming cup of coffee or tea. The tartness of lemon and sweet bite of ginger make an irresistible combination in these tender, buttery scones. There's really no need for jam or cream with them; the lemon glaze completes the flavor very nicely.

INGREDIENTS

½ cup flour

1 tablespoon plus 1 teaspoon sugar

⅛ teaspoon salt

½ teaspoon baking powder

¾ teaspoon grated lemon zest or ¼ teaspoon pure lemon extract

2 tablespoons unsalted chilled butter, diced

2 tablespoons diced candied ginger (I like using ginger tidbits available from King Arthur Flour)

¼ cup milk

1 tablespoon beaten egg

LEMON GLAZE:

1 teaspoon butter, melted

1 teaspoon lemon juice

¼ cup confectioner's sugar

DIRECTIONS

1. Preheat your oven to 375°F; shift the rack to second highest position if it's a full-sized oven. Combine the flour, sugar, salt, baking powder, and lemon zest (if you're using lemon extract, add it with the wet ingredients).

2. Cut in the butter with a fork or pastry cutter until it resembles coarse cornmeal. Stir in the candied ginger.

3. Combine the milk and beaten egg (and extract if using) and stir into the dry ingredients with a fork until it just holds together.

4. Use a ¼ cup ice cream scoop or measuring cup and place two even mounds of the dough on an ungreased baking sheet lined with wax paper or parchment paper. If desired, brush the tops with a little of the beaten egg.

5. Bake for approximately 25 minutes, until puffed and golden.

6. For the glaze, combine the melted butter, lemon juice, and confectioner's sugar and spread evenly over the warm scones. Serve warm or at room temperature.

This recipe makes two scones with a total of about 690 calories; 345 calories each.

Cranberry Orange Scones
Moderate

Cranberry and orange has become a classic flavor combination, made easy here with the addition of sweetened dried cranberries. With these or any of the other scone recipes listed here, you may substitute regular butter for the unsalted of you prefer; just omit the salt if you chose to do so.

INGREDIENTS

½ cup flour

1 tablespoon plus 1 teaspoon sugar

½ teaspoon baking powder

⅛ teaspoon salt

¾ teaspoon grated orange zest or ¼ teaspoon pure orange extract

2 tablespoons unsalted chilled butter, diced

¼ cup milk

1 tablespoon beaten egg

2 tablespoons dried cranberries

ORANGE GLAZE:

¼ cup confectioner's sugar

1 teaspoon melted butter

1 teaspoon orange juice

DIRECTIONS

1. Preheat the oven to 375°F, shifting the rack to a middle upper setting if using a full-sized oven.

2. Combine the flour, sugar, baking powder, and salt in a medium mixing bowl; if using orange zest add that as well.

3. Using a pastry cutter or fork, cut in the butter until the mixture resembles coarse crumbs. Combine the milk, egg, and, if you're using it, the extract.

4. Stir into the dry ingredients along with the dried cranberries until the mixture just holds together.

5. Scoop into two even mounds onto an ungreased baking sheet lined with wax paper or parchment baking paper. If you wish, brush the tops with a little beaten egg. Bake for about 25 minutes, until they are puffed, firm to touch, and light golden.

6. For the glaze, combine the confectioner's sugar, melted butter, and orange juice and spread evenly over the two scones. Enjoy warm or at room temperature.

There are approximately 700 calories in the entire recipe, or 350 calories per scone.

Maple Walnut Scones
Moderate

Sweet and satisfying Maple Walnut Scones will get your day off to a grand start. The walnuts add flavor and crunch, while the sweet maple glaze tops everything off nicely. Savor them with a mug of steaming coffee or glass of cold milk. If enjoying one at a time, simply place the remaining scone in a zip-lock sandwich bag to save for another day. This recipe makes two scones.

INGREDIENTS

½ cup flour

1 tablespoon plus 1 teaspoon packed brown sugar

½ teaspoon baking powder

⅛ teaspoon salt

2 tablespoons unsalted chilled butter, diced

1 tablespoon beaten egg

¼ cup milk

¼ teaspoon natural maple flavoring

2 tablespoons diced walnuts

MAPLE GLAZE:

1 teaspoon butter, melted

2 teaspoons pure maple syrup

¼ cup confectioner's sugar

Walnut halves or diced walnuts, optional

DIRECTIONS

1. Preheat oven to 400°F. Combine the flour, brown sugar, baking powder, and salt in a small mixing bowl. Work in the cold butter with your fingers until the mixture resembles coarse cornmeal.

2. Combine the egg, milk, and maple flavoring and add to the dry ingredients all at once, stirring with a fork until just well combined.

3. Divide into two equal scoops on a parchment- or wax paper–lined baking sheet that has been lightly coated with non-stick cooking spray. I find a ¼ cup ice cream scoop works very well for this purpose.

4. Bake on a middle upper rack for approximately 25 minutes, until the scones are puffed, browned, and firm to touch.

5. Combine the glaze ingredients and swirl evenly over the tops of the warm scones. If you wish, top each scone with a walnut half or a few more pieces of diced walnuts. These are especially delicious served warm.

There are about 800 calories in the entire recipe; about 400 calories per scone.

Savory Cheese and Olive Scones
Moderate

Try these when you're in the mood for a not-sweet breakfast or coffee break treat. They also make a tasty accompaniment to a variety of main course dishes, or you can enjoy them as a side with soup for lighter fare.

INGREDIENTS

½ cup flour

1 teaspoon sugar

½ teaspoon baking powder

⅛ teaspoon garlic salt

⅛ teaspoon paprika

¼ teaspoon oregano or mixed Italian herbs

1 tablespoon unsalted chilled butter

¼ cup milk

1 tablespoon beaten egg

2 tablespoons sliced olives

3 tablespoons grated Parmesan or blended Italian cheese, divided

DIRECTIONS

1. Preheat the oven to 375°F, with rack in medium high position if using a full-sized oven.

2. Combine the flour, sugar, baking powder, garlic salt, paprika, and Italian herbs or oregano in a small mixing bowl, stirring to mix well.

3. Cut in the butter, using a pastry cutter or fork, until the mixture resembles coarse crumbs. Stir together the milk and beaten egg; then stir them into the dry mixture along with the olives and 2 tablespoons of the cheese until everything is just well blended.

4. Scoop evenly onto a wax paper– or parchment-lined baking sheet; about ¼ cup each for two mounds of dough. Sprinkle with the remaining tablespoon of grated cheese and bake for approximately 25 minutes, until the scones are puffed, golden, and firm to touch. Serve warm or at room temperature.

There are about 500 total calories or 250 calories per scone.

Giant Butter Flake Biscuits
Moderate

Shredding the butter makes the process a snap, and gives just the right texture for light, delicate biscuits. Giant Butter Flake Biscuits also forms the base for Sticky Biscuit and Quick Mini Coffee Cake.

INGREDIENTS

⅔ cup flour

¼ teaspoon salt

1½ teaspoons baking powder

2 teaspoons sugar

2 tablespoons plus 2 teaspoons cold butter

⅜ cup milk

DIRECTIONS

1. In a small bowl, stir together the flour, salt, baking powder, and sugar.

2. Shred the very cold butter directly into the dry ingredients and toss lightly. Pour the cold milk over the mixture, stirring with a fork until it just holds together.

3. Gather the dough together with your hands and pat it out and fold over 3–4 times on a floured surface. Divide in half and lightly pat each half to about 1" thick, as close in size to the perimeters of your designated cutter as possible. Cut using a round cookie cutter, drinking glass, or jar neck dipped in flour, or simply hand cut around the edges. Cutting the edges allows the biscuit to rise more evenly, giving you a nice high biscuit.

4. Bake in a 375°F oven for about 20 minutes, until light golden brown. Serve hot with butter, jam, or honey.

Each plain biscuit has about 310 calories.

Sticky Biscuit

Moderate

Here's an easy to prepare variation on a sticky bun . . . yum! Add your choice of nuts, raisins, or some of each.

INGREDIENTS

1 recipe Giant Butter Flake Biscuit dough
   (p. 42)
4 teaspoons butter
¼ cup brown sugar
2 teaspoons honey or corn syrup

1 teaspoon cider vinegar
2–4 teaspoons water
¼ cup pecans, walnuts, raisins, or try half
   nuts and half raisins

DIRECTIONS

1. Prepare the biscuit dough as directed, but do not pat it out.

2. Divide the butter between two 4" pie plates and allow it to melt in the oven while it's preheating to 375°F.

3. Remove pans from oven. Add remaining ingredients to a mixing bowl, stirring to blend well.

4. Divide the biscuit dough between the two pans, and bake for about 20 minutes, until the biscuits are risen, light golden, and firm to touch.

5. Upon removing from the oven, run a knife around the edge of each biscuit and immediately turn out onto a serving plate. Be careful: the melted sugar mixture is very hot! Allow to cool about 5 minutes before enjoying.

Each biscuit is about 595 calories with pecans or 555 with raisins.

Quick Mini Coffee Cake

Moderate

This is somewhat reminiscent of the little packaged crumb coffee cakes we had as a treat when I was a kid . . . except it's really much better. Enjoy it with coffee, tea, or a glass of cold milk.

INGREDIENTS

2 tablespoons flour

2 tablespoons rolled oats

¼ cup sugar

½ teaspoon cinnamon

1 recipe Giant Butter Flake Biscuit dough (p. 42)

4 teaspoons butter, melted

DIRECTIONS

1. Combine everything but the biscuit dough and butter in a small bowl. Divide the biscuit dough between two buttered 4" pie pans.

2. Stir together the butter and other topping ingredients and sprinkle evenly over the top of the biscuit dough.

3. Bake at 375°F until golden brown and firm to touch. Remove and cut into wedges to serve; it will cut more easily if you allow it to cool slightly first.

Each mini coffee cake totals about 545 calories.

Cinnamon-Topped Blueberry Muffins
Moderate

These muffins are especially delicious made with wild blueberries, if you can find them. Wild blueberries are often available frozen; simply measure out and rinse briefly under cold running water; drain well and add to the batter. However, they are also very tasty made with larger domestic berries, which are more readily available. Either way, please don't skimp on the blueberries when making blueberry muffins; some of the commercially produced charlatans out there masquerading as blueberry muffins are truly pathetic. Not to mention, blueberries, in addition to being delicious, are a nutritional powerhouse; so go ahead, enjoy! This recipe makes two muffins.

INGREDIENTS

2 teaspoons butter, melted

2 tablespoons milk

1 tablespoon beaten egg

¼ cup flour

1 tablespoon sugar

Small dash salt

⅜ teaspoon baking powder

¼ cup blueberries

TOPPING:

2 teaspoons sugar

⅛ teaspoon cinnamon

DIRECTIONS

1. Preheat oven to 375°F.

2. Combine the melted butter, milk, and egg in a small mixing bowl.

3. Add the flour, sugar, salt, and baking powder, stirring together until just well blended. Gently stir in the blueberries.

4. Divide the mixture evenly between 2 paper-lined muffin cups that have been sprayed lightly with non-stick cooking spray.

5. For the topping, combine the 2 teaspoons of sugar with the cinnamon and sprinkle evenly over the tops of the two muffins. Bake on an upper rack, if possible, for approximately 20–25 minutes, until the muffins are puffed, golden brown, and firm to touch.

6. Allow muffins to cool slightly before enjoying; the blueberries will be quite hot when first removed from the oven. These are best eaten fresh, although they will store nicely for a couple of days. The cinnamon sugar topping will soften with time.

Total calories per recipe are about 300, or 150 calories per muffin.

Choco-nut Banana Muffins

Moderate-Complex

Mellow and rich, Choco-nut Banana Muffins are worthy of a weekend splurge. They combine many of our favorite flavors into one breakfast or brunch delight. Although mini chips work particularly well in these muffins, feel free to use whatever you have on hand. This recipe makes 4 muffins; you can easily halve it if you really only want to make two, or if you don't wish to consume them all within a couple of days, simply wrap and freeze for up to a month. Unwrap and microwave for a few seconds when you're ready to enjoy.

INGREDIENTS

½ ripe banana, peeled and mashed (3 tablespoons)

2 tablespoons hazelnut chocolate spread

1 tablespoon oil

2 tablespoons sugar

2 tablespoons milk

½ egg, beaten (2 tablespoons)

6 tablespoons flour

¼ teaspoon baking powder

¼ teaspoon baking soda

¼ teaspoon salt

4 teaspoons semi-sweet chocolate chips

4 teaspoons chopped hazelnuts

DIRECTIONS

1. Preheat oven to 375°F; move your upper rack to second position from top if using a standard oven.

2. Beat together the banana, chocolate hazelnut spread, oil, sugar, milk, and egg until the mixture is smooth.

3. Combine the flour, baking powder, baking soda, and salt and stir into the chocolate/banana mixture along with the chocolate chips and hazelnuts until well blended.

4. Divide evenly between 4 paper-lined muffin cups, spritzed with non-stick cooking spray for easy removal. Bake for approximately 20–25 minutes, until they are puffed and firm to touch. Serve warm or at room temperature.

This recipe is approximately 920 calories total; 230 calories per muffin.

Lemon Poppy Seed Muffins

Moderate

This recipe makes two delicious "normal"-sized muffins; neither the oversized extravaganzas that run over 600 calories apiece nor the mini muffins, which hardly allow you a decent mouthful. The lemon glaze adds an especially bright fresh flavor.

INGREDIENTS

1 tablespoon butter, melted

2 tablespoons granulated sugar

1 tablespoon sour cream

1½ tablespoons beaten egg

¼ teaspoon pure lemon extract

3 teaspoons lemon juice, divided

1 teaspoon poppy seeds

¼ cup all-purpose flour

Small pinch (1/16 teaspoon) baking soda

⅛ teaspoon salt

3–4 tablespoons confectioner's sugar

DIRECTIONS

1. Move upper oven rack to second from top position, if using a full-sized oven, and preheat to 400°F.

2. Combine the melted butter, sugar, sour cream, egg, lemon extract, 2 teaspoons of the lemon juice, and the poppy seeds in a small mixing bowl until well blended.

3. Combine flour, baking soda, and salt, and add to wet ingredients, mixing until just combined.

4. Divide batter between two buttered and floured or paper-lined muffin cups and bake for 20 minutes, until light golden and firm to touch.

5. Combine the remaining teaspoon of lemon juice with the confectioner's sugar. Spread the glaze evenly over the warm muffins. These may be eaten right away or a little later at room temperature.

There are 470 calories total in this recipe; 235 per muffin.

PB&J Muffins

Moderate-Complex

Who among us doesn't enjoy peanut butter and jelly? For a refreshing change from sandwiches, try these tasty muffins. A little banana added to the batter enhances the moist texture and adds subtle flavor. This recipe yields three standard-sized muffins.

INGREDIENTS

2 tablespoons peanut butter

1 tablespoon oil

½ ripe banana, mashed (2–3 tablespoons)

2 tablespoons beaten egg (about ½ egg)

¼ teaspoon vanilla extract

2 tablespoons milk

2 tablespoons packed brown sugar

¼ cup all-purpose flour

⅛ teaspoon baking powder

⅛ teaspoon baking soda

Small pinch (¹⁄₁₆ teaspoon) salt

1 tablespoon favorite jam or jelly

DIRECTIONS

1. Preheat your oven to 375°F; if using a full-sized oven, adjust the rack to the medium upper position.

2. Whisk together the peanut butter, oil, banana, and egg until smooth. Add in the vanilla, milk, and brown sugar, whisking again to dissolve any lumps in the sugar.

3. Stir in the flour, baking powder, baking soda, and salt until smooth.

4. Divide evenly between three paper-lined or greased and floured muffin cups. Spritz a little non-stick cooking spray into each muffin paper before adding the batter for easy removal.

5. Place a teaspoon of the jam on top of each muffin. Bake for approximately 20–25 minutes, until golden brown, puffed, and firm to touch. Allow the muffins to cool slightly before enjoying; the jam will be hot and the muffin itself somewhat fragile initially.

There are 490 calories total; 165 per muffin.

Honey Cornbread

Moderate

Honey Cornbread is equally tasty as a breakfast or supper dish. Try it paired with scrambled eggs and ham for a hearty morning meal, or use it to accompany Beef Stew for Two (p. 123) or Chili with Beef and Beans (p. 267).

INGREDIENTS

2 tablespoons butter, melted
½ cup milk
1 egg, beaten
2 tablespoons honey

⅔ cup flour
⅓ cup cornmeal
2 teaspoons baking powder
½ teaspoon salt

DIRECTIONS

1. Combine melted butter in a medium mixing bowl with the milk, egg, and honey, whisking until smooth.

2. Combine flour, cornmeal, baking powder, and salt, and stir into wet ingredients until everything is just well mixed.

3. Pour into a buttered 4" x 8" pan, smoothing the batter evenly. Bake at 375°F for 20–25 minutes, until it is light golden and springy to touch.

Makes four pieces at 875 calories total; 220 calories per piece.

Breakfast Buns

Complex

Here is your opportunity to enjoy a couple of sweet and buttery breakfast buns, warm from the oven, whenever you'd like it. The basic dough may be used with a variety of fillings ranging from sweet to savory to nutty. Total calories are listed with the individual fillings.

INGREDIENTS

¼ cup water

1 tablespoon plus 1 teaspoon butter

1 tablespoon plus 1 teaspoon sugar

⅛ teaspoon salt

¼ cup milk

1 teaspoon yeast

¾ cup bread flour

DIRECTIONS

1. Combine the water, butter, sugar, and salt in a small saucepan and heat to just melt the butter. Stir in the cold milk; remove from heat.

2. Once the mixture is lukewarm (a drop placed on the inside of your wrist should feel neither too hot nor too cold), stir in the yeast until dissolved, and then the flour. You will now have produced a soft, fairly sticky dough. Allow it to rest, covered, for 15–30 minutes; or you may cover and refrigerate it overnight.

3. Lightly flour a flat, non-porous surface (I use a large wooden cutting board). Divide the dough in two and pat each portion of dough down, flouring lightly only to prevent sticking. Form each portion of dough into a rectangle about 3" x 8".

4. Spread the filling of choice down the middle of each, leaving a generous edge of plain dough around all the edges. Pinch all the edges together firmly and roll the dough between your hands into a thin strip about 16"–18" long. Coil into a circle, tucking the outer end under the rest of the dough.

5. Place on a greased baking sheet and allow to rise for about ½ hour. Add your glazed topping, if called for.

6. Bake at 375°F for approximately 20 minutes, until the buns are light golden brown and sound hollow when tapped.

(continued)

7. Carefully remove from the baking sheet with a spatula. Glaze if the variation calls for this step. You may wish to let your buns cool 5–10 minutes before enjoying, as the filling will be quite hot when it's first done baking.

There are approximately 280 calories in each bun before adding any fillings.

Cinnamon Filling

INGREDIENTS

1 tablespoon plus 1 teaspoon butter   ½ teaspoon cinnamon
2 tablespoons brown sugar

GLAZE:

1 teaspoon milk or cream   4–6 drops of vanilla extract
2 teaspoons butter   4 tablespoons confectioner's sugar

DIRECTIONS

1. Cream together the butter, brown sugar, and cinnamon; use this mixture to fill the buns.

2. Prepare the glaze while the bun bakes by heating together the milk or cream, butter, and vanilla until the butter melts. Remove from the heat and stir in the confectioner's sugar until smooth. Fill and glaze as noted above.

There are 200 calories in each half of this filling and glaze for a total of 480 per bun.

(continued)

Chocolate Filling

2 tablespoons chocolate hazelnut spread or chocolate peanut butter

2 tablespoons chocolate mini chips

Cream and sugar

DIRECTIONS

1. Roll out the buns as directed in the recipe. Spread the chocolate hazelnut spread or chocolate peanut butter down the middle of the dough and top evenly with the mini chocolate chips.

2. Form as directed, brushing a little milk or cream on top and sprinkling with sugar; coarse sugar or pearl sugar are especially nice for this if you have either, although granulated works just fine as well. Bake as directed.

The chocolate filling and sugar topping equal about 185 calories per each half, for a total of 465 per bun.

Onion Filling

INGREDIENTS

1 tablespoon butter

2 teaspoons instant minced onion

¼ teaspoon garlic powder

½ teaspoon paprika

½ teaspoon seasoned salt

1 teaspoon poppy seeds

1 tablespoon water

DIRECTIONS

1. Melt the butter and stir in all the other filling ingredients.

2. Fill the buns and bake as the recipe directs. This variation is especially tasty with egg dishes or as an accompaniment to soup.

The onion filling is about 70 calories per each half, total calories about 350 per bun.

Honey Oatmeal Pan Rolls
Moderate

These easy-to-make pan rolls are a mini variation of the honey oatmeal bread I baked for years for the local farmer's market. Wrap leftovers in foil or plastic wrap or store in a lidded plastic container to eat within a day or two. If you'd like to enjoy your roll warm the next day, split and butter it before popping into the microwave for a few seconds, until the butter just melts.

INGREDIENTS

1 tablespoon butter

1 tablespoon honey

¼ teaspoon salt

½ cup hot water

¼ cup quick cooking rolled oats

1 teaspoon yeast

1 cup bread flour

DIRECTIONS

1. Combine the butter, honey, salt, and water in a small saucepan or heatproof bowl. Heat to just under boiling. Remove from heat and stir in the rolled oats.

2. Cool, stirring occasionally, to lukewarm. Stir in the yeast and allow the mixture to work for 5–10 minutes, until the yeast is nice and foamy. Vigorously stir in the flour, making a nice stiff dough. Allow it to rest, covered, for about half an hour.

3. Turn out onto a lightly floured board and knead lightly (using your knuckles and the palm of your hand to push and turn the dough over and over), until the dough is nice and elastic. If you'd like, throw a few rolled oats on the work surface at the same time; they'll adhere to the dough, giving it a little added texture.

4. Form into four even balls, rolling between the palms of your hands. Place in a well-buttered baking dish; the 6" x 4" Pyrex pan works great for this. Allow the rolls to rise for about half to three quarters of an hour, until they are almost doubled in size.

5. Bake in a preheated 375°F oven for about 25–30 minutes, until they are lightly browned and sound hollow when tapped with the back of your finger. Brush lightly with butter and turn out from pan. Enjoy at once, or cover lightly with a dish towel until you're ready to enjoy them.

This makes four rolls; approximately 680 calories total or 170 calories per roll.

Crescent Rolls

Moderate-Complex

Warm, buttery, and slightly sweet, Crescent Rolls are a classic family treat for special occasions. And as we all know, any day can be special, depending on how you look at it! Try them for breakfast or brunch topped with a dab of jam, or enjoy with dinner for a memorable accompaniment.

INGREDIENTS

1 tablespoon sugar

3 tablespoons milk

3 tablespoons butter, divided

1 teaspoon yeast

3 tablespoons warm water

1 tablespoon beaten egg

1 cup bread flour

¼ teaspoon salt

DIRECTIONS

1. Place the sugar, milk, and 2 tablespoons of the butter in a small saucepan and heat gently until the butter just melts. Remove from the heat and cool to lukewarm.

2. Meanwhile, sprinkle the yeast over the warm water, stirring to dissolve it. Combine the two liquids along with the beaten egg.

3. Using a wooden spoon or large metal spoon beat in ½ cup of the flour and the salt. Gradually add in the remaining ½ cup of flour, kneading with your hands to integrate it all and to form a smooth dough.

4. Allow it to rise, covered, in a warm, damp place for about three quarters of an hour, until it has doubled in bulk. Punch the dough down, form into a ball, and roll it out on a clean, floured surface to a circle about 12" in diameter (it will be quite thin).

5. The remaining tablespoon of butter should be very soft or melted, so that you can spread it evenly over the surface of the dough circle. Next, cut the dough crosswise in half each way, to form four triangles. Stretching the outer edges and the tip of each triangle slightly, roll it to form a crescent, curving the ends as you place each on a buttered baking sheet.

6. Allow the rolls to again rise for about three quarters of an hour. Just before baking, you may brush the tops lightly with a little more beaten egg or some milk, if you wish, for a nice golden finish.

7. Bake in a preheated 375°F oven for approximately 15 minutes, until they are golden brown and sound hollow when tapped. Serve warm or at room temperature.

The total for four rolls is 825 calories; about 210 per crescent roll.

Overnight Mini Baguettes
Moderate-Complex

This recipe makes 4 mini baguettes or 2 longer loaves. The secret to really chewy baguettes, crusty on the outside but soft within, is an extra-long rising time. This allows the gluten in the flour to more fully develop and the yeast to slowly do its job. I've started the base for this a full day in advance and never had any problems. When I try to shorten the rising time, the bread still comes out respectably enough, but it lacks the true "baguette" qualities I love. Use your discretion . . . time is on your side in this recipe!

INGREDIENTS

½ cup warm water plus ⅓ cup warm water

½ teaspoon yeast, divided

2¼ cups bread flour, divided

1 teaspoon salt

Olive oil

Cornmeal for baking pan, optional

Egg white for brushing on crust, optional

DIRECTIONS

1. Between 8 and 24 hours before you wish to eat your bread, begin your sponge starter. Use a large mixing bowl that has either a pan lid, fitted plastic cover, or a baking sheet that fits the top fairly closely (it doesn't have to be perfect). In a pinch, you can use a piece of wax paper or foil.

2. Place ½ cup of warm water, ¼ teaspoon of the yeast, and 1 cup of the bread flour in the bowl and stir it vigorously to blend it well. Cover this mixture and let it sit at room temperature for at least 4 or up to 8 hours, or in the fridge for 8 to 21 hours. It will bubble up and turn very spongy and elastic during this time.

3. Three to 4 hours before baking time, combine the remaining ¼ teaspoon of yeast, the teaspoon of salt, and 1¼ cups of flour. Add this mixture to the sponge base in the bowl along with the ⅓ cup of warm water. Mix this with a wooden spoon, the dough hook of a heavy duty mixer, and/or your hands, making sure the starter ends up thoroughly incorporated with the other ingredients. Again cover the bowl and allow it to stand at room temperature for about an hour and a half.

4. Remove the dough from the bowl and place it on a lightly oiled surface. Knead and shape it into 2–4 slightly flattened oblongs. Fold each over onto itself, tucking in the ends, and roll back and forth with your hands into a thin 6"–12" baguette loaf. Place

side by side on a lightly oiled baking sheet that has been sprinkled with cornmeal if you wish, seam sides down. Allow to rise for another hour and a half.

5. If you have a spray bottle, spritz the loaves with water; otherwise gently pat a little water onto the surface. If you have a little extra egg white, try smoothing that on as well; this helps the baguettes form nice crispy crusts. Using the sharpest knife you have, cut three angled slits in each loaf. Bake in a preheated 450°F oven until the loaves are deep golden brown, about 25–30 minutes.

6. Allow to cool in the oven, with the door open, for about 10 minutes. These may be served warm, which is delicious, or allowed to cool to room temperature for easier slicing. If you're saving one or more of the baguettes for later, be sure to cool them thoroughly before wrapping. The baguettes will have crisp crusts when fresh; chewy crusts the next day.

Each mini baguette will total about 250 calories; 500 if you choose to make 2 longer loaves.

SATISFYING SOUPS, SALADS & SANDWICHES

If you love homemade soup as much as I do, you'll understand why I've included so many recipes for it. While canned soups can provide an easy and economical meal at times, they're still just that . . . canned. All the soups listed below do start with one common ingredient: ready-made broth. Because you're only making a double serving of soup, the broth provides many of the basic flavoring ingredients, saving time and money in the preparation process. You're then able to build a variety of flavorful soups you'll never find in a can, ranging from simple to complex. So, get ready to enjoy some "souper" meals!

CHICKEN- & BEEF-BASED SOUPS

I use reduced sodium chicken broth and beef broth when preparing the following soups. Several of them incorporate ingredients that have some saltiness on their own; all benefit from being seasoned to your own preference. It's much easier to add a little salt if need be than it is to remove it once it's already in the soup.

Avgolemono (Greek Lemon Chicken Soup)

Moderate

This Mediterranean classic combines chicken and rice broth with lemon and egg to produce a savory pale yellow soup with velvety texture. Be careful not to boil the soup once you add the egg or it might curdle. Although using egg yolk alone will produce the best texture, a portion of whole beaten egg is an acceptable substitute, and a good way to use up a little leftover egg!

INGREDIENTS

2 cups reduced sodium chicken broth

1 teaspoon instant minced onion

½ bay leaf

¼ cup diced celery

2 tablespoons uncooked rice

1 boneless, skinless chicken breast portion

1 egg yolk or 1 tablespoon beaten egg

1 tablespoon lemon juice

Fresh ground salt and pepper

DIRECTIONS

1. Combine the chicken broth, onion, bay leaf, celery, and rice in a medium saucepan. Bring just to a boil.

2. Add the chicken breast, bring to a boil again, and reduce heat to medium low. Cook the chicken breast for about 10 minutes until it's just done through. Cutting it in half to check for uniform color is a good way to determine this.

3. Leave the broth simmering on the stove while you dice the chicken into bite-sized pieces. Return the chicken to the pan.

4. Beat together the egg yolk and lemon juice and stir it quickly into the simmering soup. Adjust for seasoning with salt and pepper to taste, remove the bay leaf, and serve immediately. If having a single serving, the rest may be refrigerated and later gently reheated on the stovetop or in the microwave; just don't boil it.

There are about 330 calories in all or 165 per serving in this recipe.

Coconut Chicken Soup
Moderate-Complex

This soup with an Asian flair only takes about 15 minutes to prepare. Vary the amounts of soy sauce and lime juice to reflect your personal taste. It will make two hearty servings of soup; a nice light meal, or try coupling it with Fried Rice Breakfast Patties (p. 25) or the main course of your choice. If you use reduced calorie coconut milk, you will cut about 200 calories from the total.

INGREDIENTS

1¾ cups reduced sodium chicken broth

1 tablespoon thinly sliced lemongrass

1 teaspoon minced ginger root

Dash red pepper flakes

1–2 teaspoons soy sauce

1 medium clove garlic, peeled and minced

1 boneless, skinless chicken breast portion

½ cup snow peas, halved diagonally if large

½ small red bell pepper, seeded and cut in thin strips

½ cup button mushrooms, halved

¼ cup sliced scallions

¾ cup coconut milk

2–3 teaspoons lime juice

DIRECTIONS

1. Combine the chicken broth, lemongrass, ginger, red pepper flakes, soy sauce, and garlic in a medium saucepan. Bring to a boil, reduce heat, and boil gently for 5 minutes.

2. Meanwhile, slice the chicken breast into thin strips. Add to the boiling broth, bring back to a boil, and cook another 5 minutes.

3. Add in the snow peas, red pepper strips, mushrooms, and scallions and cook another 2–3 minutes, until the vegetables are crisp and tender but still brightly colored.

4. Last, stir in the coconut milk and lime juice and bring just under boiling; serve at once.

There are 520 calories in this recipe when made with regular coconut milk; 260 per serving.

Chicken Corn Chowder

Moderate-Complex

This hearty recipe with a southwestern flavor may be prepared using fresh corn scraped from the cob, frozen whole kernel corn, or even canned; whatever is easiest for you. If you don't have evaporated milk, simply combine ⅓ cup nonfat dry milk with ½ cup water. This makes two generous servings.

INGREDIENTS

1½ cups reduced sodium chicken broth

1 teaspoon instant minced onion

½ teaspoon cumin powder

½ teaspoon paprika

¼ teaspoon salt

1 boneless, skinless chicken breast portion

½ cup whole kernel corn

½ cup peeled, diced sweet potato

2 tablespoons diced red or green bell peppers

2 tablespoons chopped fresh cilantro

½ cup evaporated milk

1 tablespoon butter

DIRECTIONS

1. Combine the broth, instant minced onion, cumin powder, paprika, and salt in a medium saucepan. Bring to a boil, add the chicken, corn, sweet potato, and peppers and heat until it resumes boiling. Reduce the heat slightly and gently boil the chicken for about 5 minutes, until it's just cooked.

2. Remove the chicken and set aside until it's cooled enough to cut into small cubes. Meanwhile, continue to simmer the soup on low heat for another 5 minutes.

3. Add the cubed chicken, cilantro, evaporated milk, and butter. Heat until the butter melts; do not boil. Serve at once. It may also be cooled and refrigerated, covered, for up to a week; simply microwave or reheat on the stovetop.

Total calories are approximately 520 per batch; 260 per serving.

Italian Wedding Soup
Moderate

Tiny meatballs and pasta float in flavorful chicken stock in Italian Wedding Soup. Bright green spinach adds color and flavor. Use the ground meat of your choice for the meatballs. This soup is especially good served with crusty bread, and perhaps a nice salad on the side.

INGREDIENTS

4 ounces lean ground beef, turkey, or chicken

¼ teaspoon garlic salt

Dash pepper

¼ teaspoon Italian herbs

1 tablespoon beaten egg

1 tablespoon fine breadcrumbs

2½ cups reduced sodium chicken broth

¼ cup diced carrots

¼ cup piccolini or orzo pasta

Grated Parmesan cheese

Fresh spinach

Salt and pepper

DIRECTIONS

1. In a small mixing bowl, combine the ground meat, garlic salt, pepper, Italian herbs, egg, and breadcrumbs, mixing well. Form into a dozen or more tiny meatballs.

2. Heat the broth and carrots to boiling; add the pasta and meatballs and reduce to a gentle boil. Cook for 8–10 minutes, until the pasta is tender and the meatballs cooked through. Season to taste with salt and freshly ground pepper.

3. Place a handful of fresh spinach in each of two soup bowls and pour the hot soup over the spinach. Sprinkle with grated cheese and enjoy.

There are 400 calories total; 200 per serving plus cheese.

Easy Borscht

Easy-Moderate

This easy take on a classic northern European soup may be made with either canned or fresh cooked beets. I find fresh beets to have a slightly sweeter flavor than canned, although the canned beets will most likely have a little added salt. Therefore, you may wish to adjust the amounts of brown sugar and salt you use accordingly. Some folks prefer their borscht left chunky; if you're one of those people, simply omit the puréeing step.

INGREDIENTS

2 cups reduced sodium beef broth

1 small can (8.25 ounces) sliced or diced beets or 1 medium beet, peeled, diced, and cooked in water to cover until tender (do not drain)

¼ cup diced carrot

½ cup diced potato

½ cup shredded cabbage

1 teaspoon instant minced onion

½ teaspoon dried dill weed or 1 teaspoon fresh chopped

1 small or ½ large bay leaf

1 tablespoon packed brown sugar

1 tablespoon cider vinegar

Salt and pepper to taste

Sour cream and/or hard cooked eggs for garnish

DIRECTIONS

1. Combine the beef broth, beets with the canning or cooking liquid, carrots, potatoes, cabbage, minced onion, dill weed, bay leaf, brown sugar, and cider vinegar in a medium saucepan. Bring to a boil, reduce heat, and simmer, covered, for about 20 minutes, until the vegetables are very tender and the flavors have melded.

2. Remove the bay leaf and carefully blend or process until smooth. Adjust seasonings with salt and pepper to taste.

3. Serve hot or cold garnished with a dollop of sour cream and/or quartered hard cooked eggs. Buttered rye toast is especially tasty with this as well.

There are 250 calories total; 125 per serving. Two tablespoons sour cream adds 50; 1 egg adds 70.

French Onion Soup
Moderate

Who can resist this restaurant classic? The hardest part of preparing this soup is slicing the onion . . . but the rewards are great.

INGREDIENTS

1 medium large yellow onion, peeled and sliced very thin

1 small clove garlic, split

1 tablespoon butter

1 teaspoon flour

2 cups reduced sodium beef broth, chicken broth, or half of each

1 tablespoon sherry or 2 tablespoons dry wine of choice or 1 teaspoon lemon juice

¼ teaspoon salt

A few grinds fresh black pepper

1 small or ½ large bay leaf

¼ teaspoon crumbled thyme

4 slices baguette type bread

2 ounces shredded Gruyère cheese or other Swiss cheese of choice

DIRECTIONS

1. Sauté the onion and half the garlic clove in the butter over medium low heat for approximately 25 minutes, until the onions are deep golden brown.

2. Stir in the flour and cook, stirring, for a minute or two longer. Add in the beef broth, sherry, wine, or lemon juice, bay leaf, thyme, salt, and pepper. Bring to a boil, reduce heat, and simmer for about 15 minutes, to blend the flavors.

3. Meanwhile, rub the remaining half clove of garlic generously on both sides of the bread. Broil for 1–3 minutes to brown one side. Flip the bread and broil the other side.

4. Pile the shredded cheese on top and broil another minute or two until the cheese bubbles; be careful not to brown it. Ladle the hot soup into two serving bowls, removing the bay leaf and garlic clove as you do so. Float two cheese croutons in each bowl and serve at once.

The soup with croutons is 670 calories per batch; 335 calories per serving.

Teriyaki Beef Soup
Moderate

Thanks to the variety of fresh vegetables involved, this soup is as colorful to behold as it is tasty to consume. It is a nice way to use up a little leftover steak or other beef; maybe even some from a special night out. Roast pork could also be used if desired, or as an alternative, season 4 ounces of lean ground beef with salt and pepper, form into mini meatballs, and sauté them in a non-stick or lightly oiled skillet. Add to the soup when you'd normally add the steak. Japanese buckwheat or Soba noodles can be found in many larger grocery stores. If you can't find them, you can substitute precooked whole wheat spaghetti instead.

INGREDIENTS

2 cups reduced sodium beef broth

½ cup water

1–2 teaspoons soy sauce

2 teaspoons packed brown sugar

1 teaspoon finely shredded ginger root

¼ teaspoon sesame oil

Pinch red pepper flakes

¼ teaspoon garlic salt

4 ounces lean strips of leftover pot roast or steak

1 teaspoon lemon or lime juice

2 tablespoons sliced scallions

¼ cup diced carrots

½ cup snow peas, strings removed and halved if large

2–3 thinly sliced red radishes

2 ounces soba noodles

DIRECTIONS

1. Combine the beef broth, water, soy sauce, brown sugar, ginger, sesame oil, red pepper flakes, and garlic salt in a medium saucepan. Bring to a boil, reduce heat, and boil gently for 5 minutes to blend flavors.

2. Add the beef, lime or lemon juice, scallions, carrots, snow peas, radishes, and noodles. Increase heat to boiling, again reduce slightly, and cook for 4–5 minutes, until the noodles are tender. Serve at once.

There are about 350 calories per batch; 175 per serving.

VEGETABLE-BASED SOUPS

In the vegetable-based soups I use regular rather than reduced sodium vegetable broth; the lighter vegetable flavor gets a little added boost that way. And, because many of them incorporate only fruits or vegetables as the main ingredients, there is in general less salt being added to these soups to begin with. Other fruit- or vegetable-based soups include Chilled Cantaloupe Soup (p. 258) and Curried Pumpkin Apple Soup (p. 280).

Cheddar Apple Chowder

Moderate

Flavors of fall blend in this hearty cheese-based soup filled with colorful pieces of red-skinned apple. Be careful not to actually cook the apple pieces; they are at their best when the flesh is still firm and the skin nice and crisp.

INGREDIENTS

1 tablespoon butter
1 tablespoon flour
¼ teaspoon dry mustard
¼ teaspoon grated nutmeg
¼ teaspoon salt

1 cup vegetable broth
½ cup apple cider or apple juice
½ cup shredded cheddar cheese
1½ cups cored diced apple

DIRECTIONS

1. Melt the butter in a small saucepan over medium heat. Whisk in the flour, dry mustard, nutmeg, and salt until the dry ingredients are well incorporated with the butter.

2. Next whisk in the vegetable broth and cider, whisking constantly until it comes to a full boil. Reduce the heat and carefully whisk in the cheese until it just melts; don't overcook or the mixture may separate.

3. Last, add in the apples, stirring with a spoon until the soup is just heated through but not boiling. The apple skins will toughen if they cook too much. Serve at once, accompanied if you wish with rye croutons.

One serving made with reduced fat cheddar and without croutons is approximately 240 calories, or 480 for the full batch; made with full fat cheddar, each serving is about 280 calories, or 560 for a full batch.

(continued)

Rye Croutons

2 slices rye bread
1 tablespoon butter
Sprinkle of onion powder, optional

DIRECTIONS

1. Lightly butter the rye bread on each side, sprinkling lightly with onion powder if you wish.

2. Brown it in a heavy skillet over medium heat, turning once.

3. Cut into ½" cubes and serve over your Cheddar Apple Chowder.

One serving of croutons is approximately 120 calories, depending on the type of rye bread used.
The full recipe equals about 240 calories.

Corn and Tomato Bisque
Moderate

The flavors of summer are in this creamy variation on a bisque. The optional sugar will enhance the tomatoes and corn, especially if the corn isn't particularly sweet to begin with. The amount of salt you add may vary depending on the saltiness of the broth and also whether or not you used canned corn. Enjoy this velvety soup as a first course, or on its own, perhaps paired with a grilled cheese or tuna salad sandwich.

INGREDIENTS

1 tablespoon butter

1 tablespoon cornstarch

1 cup corn cut from the cob or whole kernel corn

1 large tomato, seeded and diced (about 1 cup)

¼ to ½ teaspoon herbs de Provence or mixed Italian herbs

¼ to ½ teaspoon salt

1¼ cups vegetable broth

¼ cup heavy cream

Pinch of sugar, optional

DIRECTIONS

1. Melt the butter in a medium saucepan and stir in the cornstarch. Add in the corn, tomato, herbs, salt, and vegetable broth, stirring well so that the cornstarch doesn't form lumps.

2. Bring to a boil, reduce the heat, and simmer for about 10 minutes. Purée the soup, using either an immersion or regular blender.

3. Return to the pan, add the heavy cream, the sugar if you wish, and heat gently to just under boiling.

There are 510 calories per batch; 255 per serving.

Emerald Soup

Easy

This emerald green soup is dramatic to behold and a powerhouse of delicious nutrition with the added benefit of being very low in calories and gluten free. It's a great way to use up those trimmed broccoli stems you didn't want to serve with the florets but knew you shouldn't throw away. You may enjoy this soup either hot or cold.

INGREDIENTS

1½ cups vegetable broth

1½ cups chopped fresh broccoli

1½–2 cups lightly packed fresh spinach leaves
  or ¼–½ cup well-drained cooked or frozen
  thawed spinach

½ teaspoon dried dill weed

1 teaspoon parsley flakes

Dash or 2 of salt

¼ cup sour cream

DIRECTIONS

1. Combine the broth, broccoli, spinach, dill, parsley, and salt in a small saucepan. Bring to a boil, lower heat, and cook, covered, for 5 minutes, until the broccoli is crisp and tender.

2. Purée the broth in a blender or food processor until it's as smooth as you'd like. Whisk in the sour cream and serve. If you prefer, the sour cream may be dolloped on top of the soup to stir in as you eat.

Each serving is about 100 calories; full batch is about 200 calories.

Potato Leek Soup with Peas

Easy-Moderate

This is a great fall and wintertime soup, although the fresh colors and flavors almost make it seem like spring. Use a small amount of peas from a bag of frozen peas, or leftovers from a previous meal. The optional pinch of sugar enhances the flavor of the vegetables, especially if the peas you are using are a bit large. It may be eaten either as a light meal by itself or as an accompaniment to the sandwich of your choice. It's especially tasty with grilled ham and cheese.

INGREDIENTS

1 tablespoon butter

½ cup thinly sliced leeks, tender white and light green parts only

1 cup diced potatoes

2 cups vegetable broth

¼ teaspoon salt, or to taste

Dash or 2 of white pepper

½ teaspoon dried parsley flakes

½ cup fresh or frozen green peas

Pinch or 2 of sugar, optional

4 slices crisp cooked bacon, crumbled, optional

DIRECTIONS

1. Heat the butter in a small saucepan over low heat. Add the leeks and simmer, stirring occasionally, until they are softened but not browned, about 5 minutes.

2. Add in the diced potatoes, broth, salt, pepper, and parsley flakes. Increase heat, bring to a boil, and again lower the heat to medium low.

3. Boil gently, covered, until the vegetables are tender, about 5–10 minutes. Stir in the green peas and, if you wish, a pinch or two of sugar, and heat just to boiling. Sprinkle with bacon crumbles, if desired. Serve right away to ensure the green peas retain their nice bright color.

As is, one serving of Potato Leek Soup with Peas is about 155 calories. The crumbled bacon gives a heartier main dish soup and adds 70 calories per serving.

SALAD TIME

Some salads are light and full of fruit, and others are hearty dishes of meat, cheese, and vegetables. In addition to those listed here, check out Lemon Jellied Easter Eggs (p. 242), Crimson and White Jellied Salad (p. 282), Fruit Kebabs with Citrus Cream (p. 250), and Potato Salad (p. 168).

Chef's Salad Deluxe

Moderate-Complex

If you have particular vegetables you enjoy in your salad, such as bell pepper rings, sliced onions, or radishes, feel free to add them in. Use whatever bread you prefer or have on hand for the croutons. Calories for this tasty meal in a bowl may vary according to the ingredients used. An approximate count is listed below.

INGREDIENTS

1–2 tablespoons olive oil

2 slices preferred bread; rustic or Italian style is especially nice

2 handfuls of mixed salad greens or lettuce, rinsed, drained, and torn in bite-sized pieces

1 tomato, quartered, or 4 cocktail tomatoes, halved, or 8 cherry tomatoes

½ of a medium cucumber, sliced

¼ cup shredded carrots

2 hard cooked eggs, chilled, peeled, and cut into quarters

4 ounces cooked turkey, cut into strips

4 ounces lean cooked ham, cut into strips

2 ounces Swiss cheese, cut into strips

Fresh ground sea salt and black pepper

Easy Italian Dressing (recipe follows)

DIRECTIONS

1. Heat the olive oil in a small heavy frying pan. Cube the bread and fry it in the hot oil, stirring frequently, until the cubes are golden brown. Remove from heat, sprinkle with salt and pepper, and set aside.

2. Divide the salad greens between two generously sized salad or soup bowls, or use plates if you prefer. Arrange the veggies, meat, egg, and cheese as artistically as you'd like over the greens.

3. Drizzle with Easy Italian Dressing and sprinkle the croutons over all. Enjoy at once.

With lean ham and turkey and part skim Swiss cheese:
about 350 calories per serving before adding dressing and croutons.
Made with Italian bread the croutons will equal about 200 additional calories.

(continued)

Easy Italian Dressing

This is delicious on green or tossed salads as well as Chef's Salad Deluxe. It also makes a nifty marinade for steaks or skewered meats, as in Italian Beef and Veggie Kebabs (p. 119). Although you could substitute ½ teaspoon of garlic powder if you must, the fresh minced will impart much better flavor.

INGREDIENTS

4 small or 2 large clove garlic, minced (4 teaspoons)

2 teaspoons mixed Italian herbs (basil, oregano, thyme, rosemary)

2 teaspoons salt

¼ teaspoon crushed red pepper flakes

½ cup red wine vinegar

½ cup olive oil

¼ cup water

1 teaspoon instant minced onion

DIRECTIONS

1. Peel and mince the garlic finely. Place in a small bowl or shaker jar along with the herbs, salt, and red pepper flakes.

2. Add in the red wine vinegar, olive oil, and water, whisking or shaking to combine very well.

3. Store covered, in the refrigerator. Allowing this dressing to mellow overnight will make it taste even better, as the flavors will have time to blend. Whisk or shake it again before using, and don't be alarmed if the olive oil has formed a solid upper layer when you remove it from the fridge; olive oil solidifies when chilled.

Total calories for this vinaigrette type dressing are about 900 per batch; gauge partial calories according to the amount you use.

Chicken Waldorf Salad

Easy-Moderate

Old-fashioned recipes utilize the powder harvested from staghorn sumac (not to be confused with poison sumac . . . two entirely different plants!) to concoct a lemony beverage. Powdered sumac is not as readily available as I wish it were; it imparts a slightly tart, citrusy flavor that goes especially well with salads and poultry. If you can find it, by all means try it; otherwise, a bit of grated lemon zest will do nicely as a substitute.

INGREDIENTS

2 boneless, skinless chicken breast portions (or use 1½–2 cups leftover cooked chicken)

1 cup chicken broth or water

2 crisp apples, cored and coarse diced (leave on the skin) (about 2 cups)

¼ cup thinly sliced celery

¼ cup dried cranberries

¼ cup chopped walnuts, toasted

⅔ cup seedless grapes

¼ cup mayonnaise

¼ cup sour cream or plain Greek style yogurt

2 teaspoons sugar

½ teaspoon sumac or grated lemon zest, optional

DIRECTIONS

1. Cook the chicken breast in about 1 cup chicken broth or water that has been seasoned with a pinch each of salt and pepper for about 5–7 minutes, until it's just done through. Allow to cool thoroughly and cut into 1" pieces.

2. Combine the chilled chicken with the apples, celery, dried cranberries, walnuts, and grapes.

3. In a small bowl stir together the mayonnaise, sour cream or yogurt, sugar, and sumac or lemon zest until well combined. Gently toss with the chicken and apple mixture.

4. Serve garnished with extra grapes and apple slices if you wish, or mound onto leaf lettuce.

This salad is about 650 calories per serving.

Individual Ambrosia Salads

Easy

Little containers of fruit come in handy for constructing these simple but tasty salads. If you prefer using up that partial can of pineapple or orange sections you had hanging around instead, that will be fine, too.

INGREDIENTS

1 individual container pineapple tidbits

1 individual container mandarin orange slices

2 tablespoons flaked coconut

¼ cup mini marshmallows

¼ cup sour cream

2 maraschino cherries, optional

DIRECTIONS

1. Drain the pineapple and oranges thoroughly. Add to a small bowl with everything else except the maraschino cherries, stirring to combine well. If you wish, the ambrosia may now be refrigerated, covered, until you're ready to eat it.

2. At serving time, divide between two serving dishes, top each with a cherry, and enjoy.

There are 300 calories in all, or 150 in each serving.

Strawberry Spinach Salad
Easy

Welcome in spring with this bright and cheery first course or accompaniment salad. And, since fresh spinach and strawberries are increasingly easy to find year round, lucky us! We can enjoy it whenever we please.

INGREDIENTS

2 handfuls of baby spinach leaves

4–6 large strawberries, sliced, or more if small

2 slices Swiss cheese, diced

¼ cup Lemon Poppy Seed Dressing

DIRECTIONS

1. Place one handful of spinach leaves on each of two salad plates or bowls. Arrange the strawberries on top and sprinkle the diced cheese over all.

2. Just before serving, drizzle with the dressing.

The salad alone gets most calories from the cheese; the spinach and strawberries are only about 30 per serving; the cheese may range from 70–110 depending on brand and size of slice.

Lemon Poppy Seed Dressing

INGREDIENTS

¼ cup lemon juice

2 tablespoons honey or maple syrup

2 teaspoons poppy seeds

¼ teaspoon onion powder

Dash salt

½ cup olive oil

DIRECTIONS

1. Combine the lemon juice, honey or maple syrup, poppy seeds, onion powder, and salt in a small mixing bowl or shaker jar, whisking or shaking until the thicker and thinner liquids have amalgamated.

2. Add the olive oil and again whisk or shake until the dressing is slightly thickened and everything is well combined.

The dressing contains about about 75–80 calories per tablespoon.

Tuna Macaroni Salad in Veggie Shells

Moderate

Variations on macaroni salads are always welcome during hot summer weather. This tasty tuna salad has the added benefit of being served in an edible "bowl." It's great accompanied by crusty bread or rolls. Finish it off with fruit sorbet for a light and flavorful meal.

INGREDIENTS

½ cup uncooked macaroni or other favorite pasta

½ cup fresh or frozen green peas

2 (3-ounce) individual-sized light water packed tuna

2 tablespoons sliced ripe olives

2 teaspoons snipped chives or 1 teaspoon instant minced onion

2 teaspoons lemon juice

½ teaspoon lemon pepper seasoning

Pinch or 2 of dried dill weed or 1 teaspoon fresh snipped

¼ cup mayonnaise

1 bell pepper, stem and seeds removed or 2 large tomatoes, cored and scooped out

Sliced cucumbers for garnish

DIRECTIONS

1. Cook the macaroni according to package directions. About 2 minutes before it's done, add in the green peas to heat them through but not fully cook.

2. Drain the pasta and peas, submerge them in cold water, and drain again, using a fine sieve or colander so the peas don't slip through and escape.

3. Add the tuna, olives, the chives or onion, lemon juice, lemon pepper seasoning, and dill weed.

4. Stir in the mayonnaise, mixing lightly. Pile the salad into the prepared vegetable shell. Garnish with sliced cucumbers and serve.

There are about 460 calories per serving when using a half bell pepper; about 475 when using a tomato.

SANDWICHES ARE WONDERFUL

There's a song about sandwiches that declares them to be just that. And, considering how tasty a good homemade sandwich can be, I really couldn't argue with it! Sandwiches here run the gamut from hot to cold, vegetarian to full of meat. For a fancy take on a breakfast or brunch sandwich, try Croque Monsieur or Madame (p. 259). If you're in the mood for a burger, check out Burger Deluxe (p. 251). And last, there are the bread-based entrées that aren't sandwiches . . . homemade pizza and calzones . . . right here in this chapter.

Cali Crabmeat Sandwich

Easy

This makes a colorful sandwich, bursting with fresh flavor. It's hearty enough to make a meal all in itself. Vary the amount of crabmeat as you wish; for the smaller amount, you may wish to slightly reduce the amount of celery and mayonnaise as well.

INGREDIENTS

4–6 ounces lump crabmeat
¼ cup diced celery
¼ cup mayonnaise
2 ciabatta rolls, split

Sliced tomato
Sprinkle lemon pepper seasoning salt
Avocado Cilantro Spread
Lettuce leaf

DIRECTIONS

1. Mix together the crabmeat, celery, and mayonnaise. Spread this on the base of the ciabatta rolls.

2. Top with the sliced tomato; sprinkle lightly with the lemon pepper seasoning salt.

3. Spread the avocado cilantro spread on the top half of the ciabatta rolls.

4. Add the lettuce leaf and put the sandwiches together. Skewer your sandwiches and cut in half for easy eating.

There are about 680 total calories per sandwich.

Avocado Cilantro Spread

INGREDIENTS

1 ripe Hass avocado
1 tablespoon lime juice

⅛ teaspoon salt
2 tablespoons chopped fresh cilantro leaves

DIRECTIONS

1. Mash the peeled and pitted avocado, adding in the lime juice, salt, and chopped cilantro. This spread can also be used as a dip with tortilla chips.

260 calories total in the spread.

Cuban Pork Sandwich

Easy

If you have a panini press, you can cook your sandwich right in that. I don't happen to own one, and find cooking my Cuban in a cast-iron skillet right on top of the stove works just fine, too.

INGREDIENTS

2 mini baguettes or 6"–8" sandwich rolls, split

Dijon or yellow mustard

4 ounces thinly sliced cold Cuban Roast Pork (p. 146)

2 ounces thinly sliced ham

2 ounces sliced Swiss style cheese

Thinly sliced dill pickles

DIRECTIONS

1. Spread the rolls or baguettes thinly with mustard.

2. Layer the pork, ham, cheese, and pickles evenly over the bread and close the sandwiches.

3. Grill using a panini press or a heavy skillet set over medium heat, pressing the sandwich down firmly as it cooks. You'll know they're done when the cheese has melted and the bread is crusty brown on both sides. Cut in half to enjoy.

There are about 540 calories in 1 sandwich.

Fondue on a Bun

Moderate

If you like fondue, you'll love Fondue on a Bun. It has all the gooey richness associated with classic cheese fondue, but starts with a foolproof base that won't curdle or separate at the slightest provocation. Once it's piled on the bun and lightly broiled, it's ready for fondue accompaniments of choice. This sandwich is substantial enough to feed two.

INGREDIENTS

1 mini baguette or kaiser roll, halved lengthwise

1 tablespoon butter

A thin sliver of fresh garlic or ⅛ teaspoon garlic powder

Pinch of dry mustard powder or ½ teaspoon Dijon mustard

Small pinch of nutmeg

2–3 grinds black pepper

1 teaspoon flour

¼ cup white wine

4 ounces Gruyère cheese, grated (1 cup)

OPTIONAL TOPPINGS:

broccoli florets, raw or blanched; whole or sliced mushrooms, sliced apples or pears, seedless grapes

DIRECTIONS

1. Lightly toast the baguette or kaiser roll; set aside.

2. In a small saucepan over low heat, melt the butter with the slivered garlic. Heat gently for a minute or 2 to soften the garlic and blend the flavors; don't brown it. (If you're using garlic powder, add the powder along with the other seasonings and omit this step.)

3. Next, add the mustard, nutmeg, pepper, and flour, stirring until the mixture bubbles. Add in the wine and heat just until thickened. Remove from the heat and allow the mixture to cool to room temperature; because you're working with such small amounts, this won't take very long, but it is important for the texture of the dish.

4. Lightly fold in the grated cheese and pile it on the toasted bread. Broil until the cheese mixture just bubbles but doesn't brown. Top as desired and serve at once.

There are 830 calories in the double sandwich before toppings, many of them from the cheese, which is why it will serve 2, cutting those calories down to 415 per serving.

Mini Muffalettas with Homemade Giardiniera

Complex

Once you've concocted the Giardiniera mix, it will keep fresh for several batches of Muffalettas. Store it covered, in the refrigerator. That's really the only complex element to this classic zesty sandwich; everything else just falls into place.

INGREDIENTS

¼ cup Giardiniera

1 tablespoon sliced Kalamata olives

1 tablespoon sliced green stuffed olives

1 tablespoon olive oil

2 mini baguettes or sub rolls

2 ounces thinly sliced hard salami

3 ounces thinly sliced ham

2 ounces thinly sliced provolone cheese

DIRECTIONS

1. Combine the Giardiniera with the olives and olive oil. Layer this mixture evenly on either side of the split baguettes, then add the meats and cheese in the middle.

2. Wrap each sandwich in foil and refrigerate, weighted down if possible with something heavy such as a small cast-iron skillet or a container filled with water (making sure it doesn't leak!).

3. Allow an hour or 2 for the flavors to blend; longer is fine. These are great sandwiches to take along on a picnic or to a sporting event; keep them in the foil for eating so the filling doesn't spill out!

Two sandwiches have about 1080 calories; or 540 for one.

Giardiniera (Spicy Italian pickled vegetables)

INGREDIENTS

1 cup white vinegar

1 tablespoon salt

⅛ teaspoon celery seed

Pinch of red pepper flakes

½ teaspoon oregano

1 bay leaf

1 cup tiny cauliflower florets

1 medium carrot, diced (½ cup)

1 medium stalk of celery, diced (¾ cup)

½ medium bell pepper, diced

4 pepperoncini, sliced and stems discarded

DIRECTIONS

1. Heat together the vinegar, salt, celery seed, red pepper flakes, oregano, and bay leaf to just under boiling.

2. Add in the diced vegetables and simmer for about 5 minutes. Cool completely before packing in a lidded container. This will store in your fridge for quite a long time, due to the high acid and salt content.

These vegetables are 90 calories total for 2¼ cups; 10 calories for ¼ cup.

Sunnyside Egg Club Sandwich
Easy

This simple recipe combines two sandwich favorites: egg salad with bacon, lettuce, and tomato. It's especially tasty served the classic way, accompanied by dill pickles and potato chips. I prefer only two slices of bread for this sandwich, although if you wish to sneak a third slice in there, no one will prevent you.

INGREDIENTS

2 hard cooked eggs

2 tablespoons mayonnaise

Minced celery, optional

Seasoned salt or salt and pepper

4 slices whole grain or other preferred bread

Leaf lettuce

4–6 slices ripe tomato

6 slices crisp cooked bacon

DIRECTIONS

1. Hard cook the eggs by submerging them in cold water. Heat to boiling, turn off the heat, and allow the eggs to stand, covered, for 10 minutes. Drain off the water and replace it with cold to cool the eggs down quickly.

2. Peel and dice the hard cooked eggs, mixing them with the mayonnaise, celery, and seasoned salt or salt and pepper to taste.

3. For each sandwich, spread the egg salad on one slice of the bread, or divide it thinly between both slices if you'd like the other fillings to adhere a little better. Add in the lettuce, tomato, and bacon, seasoning with a little more salt and pepper. Skewer with toothpicks if desired, cut, and enjoy.

Filling ingredients total about 270 calories per sandwich; check your bread label to determine those calories.

Squirrel Country Club Sandwich
Moderate

Who among us doesn't enjoy a peanut butter and jelly sandwich now and again? However, there's no need to relegate ourselves to a mere smear of peanut butter topped with a glob of jelly. We're adults . . . we deserve something a bit more sophisticated! And, if there happens to be a younger person in the household, here's the perfect opportunity to broaden his or her palate in a subtly delicious way! You may substitute vanilla or honey yogurt for the plain yogurt and honey, if you wish.

INGREDIENTS

2 tablespoons plain Greek yogurt

2 teaspoons honey

Pinch of cinnamon

½ cup finely shredded cabbage

2 tablespoons diced dried dates

2 tablespoons chopped salted peanuts or cashews

6 slices whole grain bread

¼ cup peanut butter or cashew butter

2 tablespoons strawberry fruit spread

1 banana, sliced

Fresh strawberries for garnish, optional

DIRECTIONS

1. Combine the yogurt, honey, and cinnamon until smooth.

2. Stir in the cabbage, dates, and cashews or peanuts.

3. For each sandwich, spread one slice of bread on one side with a tablespoon of the cashew or peanut butter. Spread a second slice of bread on one side with the strawberry fruit spread. Sandwich the sliced bananas in between these two pieces.

4. Pile the cabbage mix on top of the plain side of the strawberry spread slice. Spread the remaining cashew or peanut butter on the third slice of bread and place, spread side down, on top of the cabbage.

5. Cut diagonally into fourths, using long toothpicks skewered with fresh strawberries to hold together the four quarters, if you wish. Enjoy with a chilled glass of your finest milk.

One sandwich contains 715 calories not including fresh strawberries, when using a type of whole grain bread, which is quite tasty but also 100 calories per slice. By using reduced calorie whole grain bread, you could easily cut almost 200 calories from the total.

PIZZAS & SUCH

Time for that other take on bread and fillings . . . or toppings . . . pizza and cal-zones! It's surprisingly easy to make your own at home, ensuring fresh hot pizza with your choice of toppings for a fraction of the cost of take-out. If you don't wish to venture into the land of pizza dough you can always buy some pre-made, although since this version can be made in advance and refrigerated it's pretty much as easy . . . and has the advantage of tasting a whole lot better. There's even a recipe for pizza that's great breakfast fare: Ham and Egg Pizza. Note that the dough recipe makes enough for two individual-sized crusts, but the topping recipes make enough for one pizza. This is so it's easy to customize toppings to your individual tastes!

Individual Pizza Dough
Easy

This recipe makes two individual-sized pizza crusts and is easy to multiply, if you wish to make more than two pizzas at a time or in order to have extra dough for another day. To save the raw dough, seal in a plastic bag and refrigerate. Plan to use within 3 days.

INGREDIENTS

1 teaspoon sugar

½ teaspoon salt

1 teaspoon dry yeast

½ cup warm water

1 cup plus 2–4 teaspoons bread flour

DIRECTIONS

1. Dissolve the salt, sugar, and yeast in the warm water.

2. Beat in 1 cup of the flour to make a stiff batter. Gradually knead in enough more flour to form a soft, pliable dough. Be cautious not to make it too stiff.

3. Allow the dough to relax in the mixing bowl for at least half an hour, or place it in a plastic food bag and refrigerate it overnight.

4. Meanwhile, if eating right away, prepare the desired toppings and preheat your oven to 450°F; you want it to be good and hot when the pizza goes in. When the pizzas are prepared, bake as directed for each recipe.

Each crust has about 250 calories before toppings; the full recipe has about 500 calories.

Classy Combo Pizza

Easy

Here's a little heartier take on pizza. With lots of toppings and cheese, a single pizza could even be split between two, if you wish.

INGREDIENTS (PER PIZZA)

2 teaspoons olive oil, divided

½ recipe Individual Pizza Dough (p. 98)

3–4 tablespoons pizza or spaghetti sauce of choice

½ cup low fat shredded mozzarella cheese

4 thin slices hard salami or 8–12 slices pepperoni

4 canned artichoke quarters, drained

4 thin rings of red bell pepper

DIRECTIONS

1. Preheat your oven to 450°F; the hotter it is when your pizza goes in, the better.

2. Place about 1 teaspoon of olive oil in a 9" round cake pan, spreading it out evenly. Begin stretching the dough out a little at a time before placing it in the pan. Continue to push it out to the edges of the pan, turning it over once so that both sides are coated with the oil.

3. Spread the sauce evenly over the surface and sprinkle with the mozzarella. Place the salami in an overlapping circle on top of the cheese, or distribute the pepperoni evenly over all.

4. Space the artichoke quarters spoke-like over the surface and intersperse with the pepper rings. Drizzle with the remaining olive oil.

5. Place in the preheated oven and bake for approximately 10 minutes, until the crust is lightly browned and the cheese is bubbly. Serve hot or warm.

There are about 760 calories total; 380 per half or 165 per quarter pizza.

Pizza Margherita

Easy

This is a deliciously fresh tasting pizza easily concocted from simple ingredients. It's a perfect summertime lunch or light supper. Some of us have even been known to heat up leftovers for breakfast. My toaster oven is large enough to accommodate a 9" cake pan. If yours is not and you don't have access to a full-sized oven, you may divide the dough and toppings between two smaller pans instead.

INGREDIENTS (PER PIZZA)

3 teaspoons olive oil, divided

½ recipe Individual Pizza Dough (p. 98)

1 medium tomato, diced

Fresh ground black pepper

Garlic salt or sea salt

½ cup shredded mozzarella cheese

3–4 fresh basil leaves

DIRECTIONS

1. Preheat your oven to 450°F; the hotter it is when your pizza goes in, the better.

2. Place about 1 teaspoon of olive oil in a 9" round cake pan, spreading it out evenly. Begin stretching the dough out a little at a time before placing it in the pan. Continue to push it out to the edges of the pan, turning it over once so that both sides are coated with the oil.

3. Cover the surface evenly with the diced tomato, sprinkling it with garlic salt or salt and pepper to taste. Spread the cheese over the top of the tomatoes and place on the middle rack of your preheated oven for about 8 minutes, until the cheese is melted but not too bubbly.

4. Quickly tear the basil leaves over the top of the pizza and sprinkle with the remaining olive oil. Return to the oven for 2–3 minutes longer, until it's bubbly and the basil is barely wilted. This is best served at once, while nice and hot.

The dough contributes approximately 250 calories and the toppings 190 when using reduced fat mozzarella cheese, for a total of 440 calories per pizza.

Ham and Egg Pizza
Easy-Moderate

Ham and eggs needn't be just for breakfast, although if you'd prefer to enjoy this tasty pizza first thing in the morning, feel free! This recipe also makes a quick lunch or supper, adding in a salad if you wish to round out the meal. Since it's at its tastiest when the egg yolk is still runny, make sure you use the freshest eggs possible from a reliable source.

INGREDIENTS (PER PIZZA)

½ recipe Individual Pizza Dough (p. 98)

2 teaspoons olive oil, divided

6 tablespoons shredded cheddar cheese, or use half each cheddar and mozzarella

3 slices thin cut smoked ham, about 1½ ounces, halved

¼ cup sliced cooked asparagus, or four 4" long steamed asparagus stalk, or ¼ cup cherry tomatoes

1 fresh raw egg

Fresh ground sea salt and black pepper

DIRECTIONS

1. Preheat the oven to 450°F; adjust rack to middle.

2. Place about 1 teaspoon of olive oil in a 9" round cake pan, spreading it out evenly. Begin stretching the dough out a little at a time before placing it in the pan. Continue to push it out to the edges of the pan, turning it over once so that both sides are coated with the oil.

3. Sprinkle with the shredded cheese and place the halved slices of ham in spoke fashion on top of the cheese.

4. Place the asparagus or cherry tomatoes evenly over the ham and cheese.

5. Bake on a middle shelf for about 8 minutes; it will be mostly cooked through, with the center still soft.

6. Use a spoon to make a round egg-sized depression in the middle of the pizza. Break the egg carefully into a small bowl and slide it gently into the depression. Don't worry if a little of the white escapes; it will all cook up and be delicious anyway.

7. Sprinkle the egg with salt, pepper, and the remaining olive oil. Return to the hot oven for 2–3 more minutes, until the egg white is opaque and firm but the yolk is still soft and jiggles when gently shaken.

8. Remove to your serving plate, cut in halves or fourths, and eat immediately so that you can enjoy sopping up the egg yolk with the warm pizza crust.

This equals about 630 calories per pizza; 315 per half.

Salami and Cheese–Filled Calzone
Moderate

There are many variations to this pizza-baked-in-a-sandwich. In this variation, creamy ricotta blended with other cheeses and herbs nestles with salami inside the crust, waiting to be dunked in Tomato Dipping Sauce.

INGREDIENTS (PER CALZONE)

¼ cup part-skim ricotta

2 tablespoons shredded Parmesan cheese

1 tablespoon beaten egg plus a bit more for topping, divided

⅛ teaspoon Italian herbs

A few grinds black pepper

½ portion Individual Pizza Dough (p. 98)

1 ounce reduced fat hard salami, thinly sliced

¼ cup shredded mozzarella or provolone and mozzarella blend cheese

Non-stick cooking spray and cornmeal for dusting baking pan

DIRECTIONS

1. Combine the ricotta, Parmesan, 1 tablespoon beaten egg, herbs, and black pepper in a small bowl.

2. Roll or pat the dough out into roughly an 8" circle and transfer to a lightly oiled baking sheet.

3. Smear the ricotta filling over half the dough, leaving about 1" around the edges. Top with a layer of the salami and sprinkle with the mozzarella.

4. Fold the dough over in half, pinching the edges together and crimping them firmly with your fingers. Brush with a little egg and cut a slit in the top to allow steam to escape.

5. Bake at 425°F for 25–30 minutes, until deep golden brown. You may wish to allow your calzone to cool a bit before eating, as the filling will be quite hot. Serve with Tomato Dipping Sauce.

There are about 560 calories in 1 calzone.

(continued)

Tomato Dipping Sauce

INGREDIENTS

½ cup chopped tomato

Sprinkle each garlic powder and red or black pepper

½ teaspoon dried onion flakes

⅛ teaspoon salt

1½ teaspoons olive oil

⅛ teaspoon Italian herbs

DIRECTIONS

1. Combine everything in a small saucepan and heat gently to boiling. Reduce heat and simmer for about 5 minutes to blend flavors.

About 80 calories total in the sauce.

ENTICING ENTRÉES

This section has been divided into several categories according to the type of entrée being prepared. It begins with recipes using beef and then progresses on to chicken, pork, and seafood. Last on the list is a combination of vegetarian entrées and side dishes. The proteins in each dish have been chosen for their ease of use in small batch cooking. For the most part, small casserole dishes or the 3 cup Pyrex baking pan will be the right size for the casserole-type dishes, while a large saucepan or skillet may work better with some of the stovetop meat entrées.

BEEF & GROUND BEEF

In a smaller household, that pound of ground beef or 3 pound pot roast may seem a little too daunting for your menu. Fear not; your days of eating a hamburger a night for four days in a row are now over! We begin with a variety of ground beef dishes, each using just 4 to 8 ounces of beef. The recipes are gauged to provide one, two, or three servings each, and to give you lots of flavorful options to choose from. We then move on to a quartet of flavorful recipes utilizing chuck or flank steak (rather than purchasing a too-large pot roast), as well as a homemade-for-two version of Chicken Fried Steak.

In addition to the options that follow, see also Burger Deluxe (p. 251), Chili with Beef and Beans (p. 267), and Italian Wedding Soup (p. 67). If you're not a huge beef eater, but were brave enough to read this segment anyway, feel free to substitute ground turkey or another favorite ground meat in place of the beef.

Beef Lasagna
Easy-Moderate

Nothing hits the spot when you're hungry like a nice hot serving of lasagna. Using your favorite prepared marinara sauce cuts down on preparation time if you wish to substitute it for the tomato paste–based sauce. If you choose to use this option, plan on about 1½ cups of sauce before adding cooked ground beef. This recipe makes two hearty servings; I find one batch serves my husband and me quite nicely with a third serving left over for another day.

INGREDIENTS

6–8 ounces 85% lean ground beef

1 tablespoon instant minced onion

¼ teaspoon garlic powder

½ teaspoon salt

1 teaspoon Italian herbs

A few grinds of black pepper

6-ounce can of tomato paste

3 tomato paste cans of water or 2 cans of water and 1 can of red wine

2 lasagna noodles

¾ cup part-skim ricotta

2 tablespoons grated Parmesan

⅛ teaspoon black pepper

⅛ teaspoon nutmeg

½ teaspoon parsley flakes

½ egg

¾ cup shredded part-skim mozzarella

DIRECTIONS

1. Place the ground beef in a medium-sized heavy skillet or frying pan, breaking it into very fine pieces.

2. Add the onion, garlic powder, salt, herbs, and pepper, and cook, stirring occasionally, until the meat loses its pink color.

3. Add the tomato paste, water, and wine (if using). Bring to a boil, reduce the heat, and simmer until the sauce is thickened and reduced in volume, about 10–15 minutes; set aside.

4. Cook the lasagna noodles according to package directions. Cut each in half crosswise.

5. Combine the ricotta, Parmesan, pepper, nutmeg, parsley flakes, and egg in a medium bowl, stirring to combine well.

6. Spoon about ¾ cup of the sauce into a 3-cup 4" x 6" Pyrex pan; lay two of the half lasagna noodles lengthwise on top of the sauce. Spoon the ricotta filling evenly over the noodles and place the remaining two noodles lengthwise over the filling.

7. Add another ¾ cup or so of sauce on top; enough to cover the lasagna noodles but not to overflow the pan. Any extra sauce can be spooned over the baked lasagna when serving.

8. Bake in a 350°F oven for 30 minutes. Sprinkle the mozzarella evenly over the top and bake for another 30 minutes, until the cheese is melted and bubbly and the filling cooked through. This will serve better if you allow it to rest for about 15 minutes before cutting.

There are about 1400 calories in the entire lasagna; slightly more if made with wine. This can provide anywhere from 2–4 servings, depending on appetites involved. It will average 700 calories each in two servings, 350 each in four, or about 470 in each of three.

Ground Beef and Vegetable Casserole

Easy

If you were one of those kids who enjoyed grilling foil-wrapped hamburgers and vegetables over an open fire, this is the recipe for you. It's simple, quick, and easy to prepare, full of flavor, and satisfying. I like the combination of Montreal Steak Seasoning and seasoned salt, but feel free to use whatever strikes your fancy, or whatever you happen to have on hand. The veggies may be sliced in a food processor, on a mandoline, or the way I do it, with a nice sharp knife and cutting board. Whatever method you use, preparation time shouldn't be more than 5 minutes, allowing you lots of time to relax or attend to other things while your meal is baking.

INGREDIENTS

3–4 thin slices of onion or 2 teaspoons instant minced onion

8 ounces 85% lean ground beef

Montreal Steak Seasoning and/or seasoned salt or freshly ground salt and pepper

1 cup thinly sliced carrots

1½ cups thinly sliced potatoes

1 tablespoon butter

DIRECTIONS

1. Use a medium-sized casserole dish for this recipe. Place the onion in the bottom of the pan; pat the ground beef evenly over the onion's surface to cover the bottom entirely. Sprinkle with Montreal Steak Seasoning or salt and pepper.

2. Spread the carrots evenly over the beef and then place the potatoes evenly over the carrots. Sprinkle with seasoned salt or with more salt and pepper. Dot the butter evenly over the top.

3. Cover the casserole; if the dish you're using doesn't have an ovenproof cover, place foil over the top, crimping the edges.

4. Bake at 375°F for just over one hour, until the meat is fully cooked and the vegetables are fork tender. This recipe doubles, triples, or quadruples very easily; simply use a larger pan and increase the cooking time slightly.

Each serving is approximately 440 calories; total recipe is about 880 calories.

Mini Meatloaf
Moderate

Mini meatloaf comes out moist and tasty inside, with crisp bacon and sweet savory glaze on the outside. The ingredients listed make enough meatloaf for two servings and are easily doubled if you'd like some extra for another day. Mashed or baked potato goes especially well with this, accompanied by your favorite side vegetable. Bake your potatoes right along with the mini loaves; it will be ready at the same time. Celery seeds add a distinctive flavor to the glaze, although if you don't have any on hand, don't worry; it will be fine without them.

INGREDIENTS

2 tablespoons rolled oats

2 tablespoons beaten egg (½ egg)

½ teaspoon salt

Dash or 2 of pepper

¼ teaspoon mixed Italian herbs or oregano

4 tablespoons minced onion or 4 teaspoons instant minced onion

2 tablespoons diced bell pepper

4 tablespoons milk or water

8 ounces 85% lean ground beef

1½ teaspoons Worcestershire sauce

2 slices bacon, halved crosswise

GLAZE

2 tablespoons ketchup

1 tablespoon brown sugar

2 teaspoons prepared mustard

A few celery seeds, optional

2 shakes Tabasco sauce

DIRECTIONS

1. Combine the oats, egg, seasonings, onion, peppers, and water or milk in a mixing bowl. Allow them to sit for about 5 minutes so that the oats begin to absorb the liquid.

2. Add in the ground beef and mix lightly but thoroughly until well combined. Form into two 3" x 5" ovals and place on an ungreased baking sheet, spacing them at least 2" apart.

3. Arrange the half slices of bacon in a cross over the loaves, tucking the ends under if you can. Bake at 400°F approximately one hour, until the bacon seems fairly well cooked and the meatloaf's surface is browned.

4. Combine the glaze ingredients and pour evenly over the meatloaves. Continue to bake for another 5–10 minutes, until the loaves are nicely glazed. Allow to rest for about 5 minutes before removing carefully from the baking sheet with a spatula.

Each meatloaf contains about 320 calories when made with 85% lean ground beef.

Stuffed Peppers

Moderate

Stuffed peppers are a tasty and economical way to serve a hearty meal; two large servings use only a few ounces of meat. Use your favorite ground meat for the filling; the calorie count listed here uses 85 percent lean ground beef. The smoked cheese blend adds nice flavor, although if you prefer you can simply substitute plain mozzarella instead.

INGREDIENTS

2 tablespoons uncooked rice

1 tablespoon instant minced onion

4–6 ounces 85% ground beef

1 tablespoon drained capers, optional

½ teaspoon mixed Italian herbs

¼ teaspoon garlic powder

½ teaspoon salt

⅛ teaspoon pepper

1 egg

1 cup diced tomato

½ cup shredded smoked mozzarella/
   provolone blend cheese, divided

1 large bell pepper, halved and seeded

DIRECTIONS

1. Place the rice, onion, and ¼ cup water in a small saucepan; cover tightly and bring to a boil. Turn off the heat and allow it to sit for about 5 minutes to allow the rice to partially cook.

2. Meanwhile, combine the meat, capers, herbs, garlic powder, salt, and pepper in a medium mixing bowl. Add the egg, tomato, half the cheese, and the onion/rice mixture and mix well; your hands will accomplish this more easily than trying to use a spoon.

3. Divide the meat mixture evenly between the two bell pepper halves and place on a small baking sheet or cake tin. Bake one hour at 375°F; sprinkle on the remaining ¼ cup of cheese and bake 5 minutes longer.

   There is a total of 730 calories in the pair of stuffed peppers, or 365 calories for each half.

STEAKS TO ROASTS

We all know how delicious (and expensive) a prime cut steak can be. One of those pricier steaks is featured in Steak and Mushrooms (p. 227). However, for everyday fare, there's no reason why you can't convert what might otherwise be a hard-to-cut steak into a tender and flavorful meal. Economical varieties of beef are sold as steaks as well as roasts, and respond well to the slow cooking methods often used with the larger cuts of meat. With the exception of Chicken Fried Steak (p. 121), which utilizes cube steak, the following recipes transform those tough little steaks into savory kebabs, pot roasts, and stews through the wonders of marinating and braising. Leftover bits of cooked beef may also be utilized in Teriyaki Beef Soup (p. 70).

Classic Pot Roast

Moderate

Here's some old-fashioned comfort food for you to enjoy. Although an entire chuck roast might be too much meat for one or two, a chuck steak can be just right. And, because it weighs less to begin with, there is less cooking time involved. A side of mashed potatoes is my go-to go-with whenever there is pot roast involved.

INGREDIENTS

2 teaspoons oil

1 pound thick cut chuck steak

Black pepper, rosemary, and garlic powder

1 medium or ½ large onion, peeled and sliced

1 teaspoon salt

2 cups peeled and sliced carrots

1 tablespoon flour

DIRECTIONS

1. Heat the oil in a large skillet or saucepan. Season the meat on one side with a sprinkle each of pepper and rosemary. Brown in the hot oil; add in the onions, season the other side of the meat, and brown that as well. By the time you're done, the meat should be a nice dark brown on both sides and the onions golden.

2. Sprinkle with a little garlic powder and the teaspoon of salt and add about 2 cups of water, to just cover the meat. Bring to boiling, cover, and reduce the heat to medium low.

3. Braise the pot roast for 30 minutes. Turn it over, add the carrots, and continue to braise for another 30 minutes. Check to make sure the water hasn't cooked entirely away, adding a little if necessary; it's all right to let it reduce somewhat but you don't want to burn the pot roast. Chuck steak tends to be rather tough, so an additional half hour or so of cooking time may be in order. Once it seems fork tender, remove the meat and carrots to a serving plate.

4. Stir the flour into about ½ cup of water and stir it into the pan juices until they are bubbly and thickened. Serve the gravy with the pot roast and Creamy Mashed Potatoes (p. 165).

Chuck steak has up to 300 calories in a 4-ounce serving, although you can trim some of these by cutting away excess fat. When adding in the carrots and gravy, plan on an additional 75 calories for 3 servings or 55 calories when serving 4; the mashed potatoes will add another 160 calories per serving.

Pot Roast Provencal
Moderate

Flank steak is another good choice when preparing pot roasted meat. It's leaner than chuck and requires slightly less braising time. The ingredients in Pot Roast Provencal are a little more sophisticated than those of the classic version, and while it is delicious with mashed potatoes you could also accompany it with roasted potatoes or buttered noodles.

INGREDIENTS

1 pound thick cut flank steak
2 teaspoons oil
1 medium onion, peeled and sliced
1 medium tomato, diced
1 cup sliced mushrooms

1 teaspoon salt
½ teaspoon Herbes de Provence
Fresh ground black pepper
Water and/or red wine; about 2 cups total

DIRECTIONS

1. Brown the flank steak on both sides in the hot oil, using a heavy skillet or large saucepan. Brown the onions at the same time.

2. Add in the tomato, mushrooms, salt, herbs, and pepper. Add 2 cups of water, or 1 cup of water and 1 cup of red wine. Lower the heat to medium low and cook for about one hour, until the meat is fork tender and the vegetables have softened and formed a nice sauce.

3. Serve with your choice of accompaniment.

The flank steak has about 180 calories in 4 ounces. The vegetable sauce without wine totals about 180 calories; 60 calories for 3 servings or 45 for 4 servings. The wine doubles that to 360 calories; 120 calories for 3 servings or 90 calories for 4 servings.

Italian Beef and Veggie Kebabs

Moderate

INGREDIENTS

8 ounces lean stew beef or cubed chuck or flank steak, trimmed of excess fat

2 small or 1 medium zucchini cut in 1" slices

4 cocktail tomatoes, halved, or 8 cherry tomatoes

8 small mushrooms

Easy Italian Dressing (p. 120), to use as marinade

Herbed Rice (p. 167) or plain cooked rice

DIRECTIONS

1. Place the beef in ½ the dressing and the veggies in the remaining dressing. Cover and refrigerate for at least two hours; overnight is better.

2. If you're using wooden skewers, soak them for a half hour beforehand to prevent burning. If cooking as kebabs, thread the beef cubes onto the middle of the skewers with the zucchini, mushrooms, and tomatoes flanking them in order on either end. You may also loose broil the meat and veggies on a pan or rack with the beef in the middle and vegetables on the outer edges of the broiling area.

3. Cook your kebabs on a medium high charcoal or gas grill, turning occasionally and basting with extra, for about 10 minutes. Make sure if using dressing that marinated the meat that the juices in it have a chance to cook through by the end of your grilling/broiling time. The tomatoes will cook and soften quickly, so you may wish to thread them on near the very end.

4. Serve your beef kebabs over hot cooked rice. Any extra dressing marinade may be heated to boiling and poured over all to enhance the flavor.

One serving of the beef will account for about 260 calories and the vegetables about 40, or 300 calories total before adding the dressing/marinade. Calculate the rice calories according to which type you use.

(continued)

Easy Italian Dressing

INGREDIENTS

2 small or 1 large clove garlic, minced
  (2 teaspoons)

1 teaspoon mixed Italian herbs

½ teaspoon instant minced onion

1 teaspoon salt

⅛ teaspoon crushed red pepper flakes

¼ cup red wine vinegar

¼ cup olive oil

2 tablespoons water

DIRECTIONS

1. Peel and mince the garlic finely. Place in a small bowl or shaker jar along with the herbs, minced onion, salt, and red pepper flakes.

2. Add in the red wine vinegar, olive oil, and water, whisking or shaking to combine very well. Store covered in the refrigerator. Allowing this dressing to mellow overnight will make it taste even better, as the flavors will have time to blend. Whisk or shake it again before using, and don't be alarmed if the olive oil has formed a solid upper layer when you remove it from the fridge; olive oil solidifies when chilled. You'll use this entire recipe for marinating the beef and vegetables in Italian Beef and Veggie Kebabs. There should be plenty for two servings; if you double the kebab recipe, double your dressing recipe, too.

Total calories for this vinaigrette type dressing are about 450 per batch; gauge partial calories according to the amount you use.

Chicken Fried Steak

Easy

Chicken Fried Steak is not only real comfort food, but also surprisingly easy to whip up at home. The dredging process simply requires two shallow containers for flour and egg; seasonings are applied directly to the cube steaks to suit individual taste. Serve it with Creamy Mashed Potatoes (p. 165) and a vegetable of choice for a tasty and relaxed meal.

INGREDIENTS

Two 4-ounce cube steaks

Salt, pepper, paprika, seasoned salt, garlic salt, and/or lemon pepper seasoning

½ egg (about 2 tablespoons), beaten

2 tablespoons milk

3–4 tablespoons flour

1 tablespoon butter

1 tablespoon corn oil

¾ cup milk

DIRECTIONS

1. Sprinkle the cube steaks generously with your preferred combination of seasonings.

2. Combine the egg and 2 tablespoons of milk in one shallow container, the flour in another.

3. Melt the butter and oil together in a small, heavy skillet over medium heat. Dredge the seasoned steaks lightly in the flour, dip to cover in the egg wash, and again dredge in the flour.

4. Fry in the hot fat for 2–3 minutes per side, until the steaks are nicely browned on both sides and cooked through. Remove to serving plate and stir the remaining flour (you should have about 1 tablespoon) into the hot drippings in the skillet.

5. Cook and stir for a minute to loosen any brown bits in the bottom of the pan. Whisk in the ¾ cup of milk, allowing the gravy to bubble and thicken for a minute or two. Season the gravy to taste with salt and pepper; pour over the steaks and enjoy.

This makes two servings of chicken fried steak and gravy at about 390 calories each.

Beef Stew for Two
Moderate

Nothing hits the spot on a chilly evening like a nice bowl of homemade stew. The entire dish takes only about 1½ hours to prepare, or you could make it up to a few days early and store it, covered, in the fridge, to warm up when you're ready to enjoy it.

INGREDIENTS

2 teaspoons oil

8 ounces stew beef or chuck, top round or flank steak, trimmed of excess fat and cut in cubes

1 small or ½ large onion, peeled and chopped

1 small stalk celery, sliced thin

½ teaspoon salt, ¼ teaspoon each pepper and paprika, or ¾ teaspoon seasoned salt

½ teaspoon mixed herbs of choice

1 bay leaf

2½ cups water, divided

1 cup sliced carrots or ½ cup each sliced carrots and diced rutabaga

1½ cups red skinned potatoes, scrubbed and cut into 1" cubes

½ cup sliced mushrooms, optional

1 tablespoon flour

DIRECTIONS

1. Heat the oil in a large saucepan. Brown the steak cubes in the hot oil over medium high heat, adding in the onion and celery partway through the cooking process.

2. Add in the seasonings, herbs, bay leaf, and 2 cups of water. Bring to a boil, reduce the heat, and cook for about 15 minutes.

3. Add the carrots and rutabaga and bring to a boil again. Reduce the heat, cover, and boil gently for about 30 minutes.

4. Add in the potatoes and mushrooms, if you wish. Again bring to a boil, reduce the heat, and cook gently for another 20 or so minutes.

5. Stir the flour into ½ cup of cold water, add to the stew, and cook for an additional 5 minutes, until the gravy has thickened nicely.

6. Remove the bay leaf and serve in bowls, accompanied by pickles and bread or rolls of choice.

There are 750 calories total in this stew, or 375 per serving.

CHICKEN & POULTRY

Poultry is economical and delicious, but chances are in a smaller household you'd prefer not to be roasting an entire chicken or turkey on a regular basis. This section solves that quandary by concentrating on chicken that has already been cut up, with one set of recipes for white meat and another for dark. In addition, there are a couple of recipes dedicated to that fine little bird, the Cornish game hen. At least for now our only bow to turkey is in its precooked, smoked form.

Easy Chicken Cordon Bleu
Easy-Moderate

This variation of a classic dish is easily prepared right on top of the stove. The sweet yet slightly piquant cream sauce adds a nice finishing touch.

INGREDIENTS

2 tablespoons flour

¼ teaspoon salt

¼ teaspoon paprika

¼ teaspoon parsley flakes

Pinch or two ground red pepper flakes

2 boneless, skinless chicken breast portions

2 teaspoons butter

2 teaspoons olive oil

2 thin slices Swiss cheese

2 thin slices cooked ham

Maple Dijon Cream Sauce

DIRECTIONS

1. Combine the flour, salt, paprika, parsley flakes, and crushed red pepper in a small bowl.

2. If the chicken is individually sealed, chances are it will have a damp enough surface for dredging directly from the wrap. If the surface is too dry, simply wet it with a little cool water to facilitate the flour sticking to it. Coat the chicken well on all sides with the flour mixture.

3. Heat the butter and oil in a heavy frying pan over medium high heat until the butter foams. Add the chicken and fry for about 4 minutes per side, until it is golden brown and crispy.

4. Place a slice of Swiss cheese on top of each cooked chicken breast in the pan and place the slices of ham on top of the cheese. Carefully flip the chicken breasts over and allow the ham and cheese to heat just until the cheese melts. Carefully invert onto serving plates. Serve accompanied by Maple Dijon Cream Sauce (p. 127).

This dish with the sauce is just about 460 calories per serving.

(continued)

Maple Dijon Cream Sauce

INGREDIENTS

2 teaspoons Dijon mustard
2 tablespoons pure maple syrup
4 tablespoons sour cream

DIRECTIONS

1. Combine all the ingredients in a small bowl. When ready to serve, spoon over the chicken, or if you prefer, serve it on the side.

The sauce alone is about 105 calories per serving.

Sesame Chicken with Honey Pineapple Sauce

Moderate-Complex

This is a slightly larger recipe; it will serve 2–3, depending on the serving size desired. It is similar to, but somewhat lighter than, the dish of the same name found in many Chinese restaurants. Cooked rice is the accompaniment of choice, perhaps with a steamed green vegetable on the side.

INGREDIENTS

Pineapple Sauce
1 tablespoon sesame seeds
2 tablespoons cornstarch
¼ teaspoon baking powder
¼ teaspoon ginger
1 teaspoon sesame oil

1 tablespoon water
2 teaspoons soy sauce
8–12 ounces boneless, skinless chicken breast
   cut in 1" pieces
¾ cup peanut oil for frying

DIRECTIONS

1. First make the Pineapple Sauce (p. 129). Once that is completed, combine the sesame seeds, cornstarch, baking powder, ginger, sesame oil, water, and soy sauce in a medium mixing bowl. They will form a kind of slurry.

2. Add in the chicken pieces and mix them around well to coat evenly. Meanwhile, heat the peanut oil in a heavy frying pan until it is quite hot but not smoking. Add in the chicken, being careful to keep the pieces separate from one another. Fry quickly, turning as needed, until they are golden brown and crispy.

3. Drain the chicken to remove excess oil (when prepared in this manner the actual oil retained in the chicken will only equal about 2 tablespoons). Mix the hot fried chicken pieces with the warm pineapple sauce and serve at once.

The entire dish without rice equals about 950 calories; 475 per 2 servings.

(continued)

Pineapple Sauce

INGREDIENTS

1 individual serving cup pineapple tidbits

2 tablespoons honey

1–2 teaspoons soy sauce

⅛ teaspoon garlic powder

Pinch red pepper flakes

2 teaspoons rice vinegar or cider vinegar

1 teaspoon cornstarch

DIRECTIONS

1. Combine the pineapple and its juice in a small saucepan along with all the other ingredients except the cornstarch.

2. Using an immersion blender, blend until the mixture is fairly smooth, or alternatively, combine in a standard blender and blend smooth.

3. Stir in the cornstarch and cook over medium heat until the mixture thickens and bubbles; remove from heat and set aside.

The sauce alone is about 210 calories total.

Chicken Satay with Coconut Rice
Complex

Boneless, skinless thighs work best here. I recommend larger sized for this recipe; 6 ounces or so each would be about right. Feel free to adjust the amount of red pepper flakes dependent on personal taste; I don't care for too much heat in my dishes, which is reflected in the recipe. Just remember, a little goes a long way. Leftover Peanut Dipping Sauce may be tossed with hot cooked pasta and garnished with minced scallions and chopped peanuts for an easy-to-prepare secondary main dish.

INGREDIENTS

1 tablespoon thinly sliced lemongrass

1½ teaspoons instant minced onion

½ small clove garlic, minced

¼ teaspoon ground turmeric

1½ teaspoons ground coriander

½ teaspoon ground cumin

Pinch of red pepper flakes

1 teaspoon diced fresh ginger

2 teaspoons soy sauce

2 teaspoons Asian fish sauce

1½ tablespoons packed brown sugar

2 teaspoons peanut oil

2 large boneless, skinless chicken thighs; about 6 ounces each

Peanut Dipping Sauce

Coconut Rice

DIRECTIONS

1. Combine everything except the chicken, dipping sauce, and rice in a blender or small food processor. Blend or process until mostly smooth and creamy. If you don't have a blender, don't worry; simply mince the garlic and lemongrass extra fine and stir everything together. Kitchen scissors will make your job easier with the lemongrass.

2. Slice the chicken into long, thin strips by laying it out as flat as possible and cutting each into four pieces. Place the chicken in a small, nonreactive bowl and pour the marinade over it, mixing to coat it well. Cover and refrigerate at least an hour or up to 24 hours.

3. Meanwhile, prepare Peanut Dipping Sauce (p. 131), which can also be stored in the refrigerator. Prepare the Coconut Rice (p. 132) just before grilling the chicken. If using wooden skewers, soak them in warm water for at least ½ hour to prevent

(continued)

burning. I use thin metal skewers, which allow me to thread an entire serving on one skewer.

4. Preheat your grill to medium high. Skewer the chicken and grill or broil, turning two or three times, until it is deeply browned and cooked through—roughly 20 minutes, depending on the grill. Serve with the Peanut Dipping Sauce, Coconut Rice, and steamed green vegetables of choice.

There are approximately 540 calories in the Satay, or 270 per serving before adding sauce and rice.

Peanut Dipping Sauce

INGREDIENTS

¼ cup natural peanut butter

1 small clove garlic, finely minced

1 teaspoon soy sauce

2 teaspoons fish sauce

1 teaspoon sesame oil

2 teaspoons lime juice

2 tablespoons packed brown sugar

Pinch of cayenne or ground red pepper flakes, to taste

¼ cup coconut milk

¼ cup water

DIRECTIONS

1. Combine everything but the coconut milk and water in a small mixing bowl and stir until smooth.

2. Add the coconut milk and water and stir or whisk until smooth.

This makes approximately 1 cup of sauce for a total of 570 calories; about 75 calories per 2 tablespoon serving. If you substitute reduced fat coconut milk, the count will go down commensurately.

(continued)

Coconut Rice

Creamy Coconut Rice provides a mellow accompaniment to the spicy Satay. Leftover Coconut Rice can easily be transformed into dessert pudding; just heat with a little milk or water and a sprinkling of cinnamon sugar. Garnish with pineapple tidbits and/or whipped cream if desired.

INGREDIENTS

½ cup jasmine rice

½ cup water

½ cup coconut milk

1 tablespoon shredded or flaked coconut

DIRECTIONS

1. Bring the rice, water, and coconut milk to boiling in a small saucepan. Stir to prevent sticking. Add the coconut, stir again, and cover tightly.

2. Turn off the heat and allow the rice to cook on retained heat for about 20 minutes, until the liquid is absorbed. Fluff the rice and serve.

This will make two ¾-cup servings at about 210 calories per serving when made with regular coconut milk. If using reduced fat coconut milk, the calories will be reduced significantly.

Stovetop Bacon Barbecue Chicken

Easy

This dish is super easy to prepare. Because it's cooked indoors, you can enjoy it any time of the year in any weather. Try Potato Salad (p. 168) as a summer accompaniment or Potatoes O'Brien (p. 261) when the weather turns chilly.

INGREDIENTS

2 (4–5-ounce) boneless, skinless chicken
  thighs
2 slices bacon

2 tablespoons honey
2 tablespoons barbecue sauce

DIRECTIONS

1. Open the chicken thighs out and wrap one slice of bacon around each, beginning and ending on the same side.

2. Place in a cast-iron frying pan and fry, covered, over medium low heat until both sides are deep golden brown and the bacon is cooked through, about half an hour, turning occasionally.

3. Combine the honey and barbecue sauce, pour over the chicken in the hot pan, and cook for just a minute longer, until the sauce caramelizes and glazes the chicken. Serve at once.

There are 275 calories per serving.

Chicken in Rustic Cream Sauce
Moderate-Complex

This recipe heats up beautifully as a leftover, if you only consume a single serving at a time. For this particular recipe bone-in thighs with the skin still on will add a more rounded flavor than boneless, skinless thighs, although either may be used.

INGREDIENTS

2 large chicken thighs
½ teaspoon Herbes de Provence
¼ teaspoon salt
A few grinds black pepper
1 tablespoon olive oil
1 clove slivered garlic
1 shallot, peeled and sliced

1 medium tomato, peeled and chopped
  (½ cup)
½ cup sliced mushrooms
1 tablespoon capers
½ cup white wine
¼ cup heavy cream
Hot cooked rice

DIRECTIONS

1. Season the chicken on both sides with the herbs, salt, and pepper. Brown it in the hot olive oil until golden all over, adding in the garlic and shallots to soften during the last part of the browning process.

2. Stir in the tomato, mushrooms, and capers and then pour the wine over all. Bring to a boil, reduce the heat, and boil gently, covered, turning once or twice, until the chicken is tender and the juices reduced by approximately half, about 35–40 minutes.

3. Add the cream to the chicken and juices in the pan, increase heat to medium high, and boil, uncovered, stirring frequently until the sauce is slightly thickened, about 5 minutes.

4. Serve the chicken and cream sauce with hot cooked rice and a green vegetable of your choice.

Total calories are about 750; or 325 per serving when the skin is removed before eating; add 80 additional calories for each ½ cup of cooked white rice.

Crispy Oven-Fried Chicken

Easy

Bone-in chicken thighs with the skin fits the bill for this recipe—an easy and economical main dish that practically cooks itself. If you don't feel like crushing cereal or don't happen to have any on hand, feel free to substitute panko or other breadcrumbs instead. Pop a couple potatoes in to bake at the same time and voilà! Dinner is served.

INGREDIENTS

2 teaspoons butter

2 teaspoons corn or other vegetable oil

2 chicken thighs

¼ cup crushed crispy rice or corn cereal

¼ teaspoon Italian herbs or other favorite herbs

Dash of paprika

Dash of garlic powder

Several grinds of black pepper

⅛ teaspoon salt

DIRECTIONS

1. In a small baking dish, heat the butter and oil together until the butter melts. Dip the chicken to coat all sides.

2. Combine all remaining ingredients, mixing well. Dip the chicken in the crumb mixture, again coating on all sides. Place back in the baking dish, skin side up.

3. Bake in a preheated 400°F oven for about an hour, until golden brown, crispy, and juices run clear when poked with a fork.

Each baked thigh will equal about 255 calories when prepared with crushed rice cereal.

CORNISH GAME HEN & TURKEY

These tiny fowl are the perfect choice for a small household, and are increasingly available year round. See also Roast Cornish Hen with Cranberry-Orange Stuffing and Glaze (p. 272). Since turkeys in general are large birds, I've only included one turkey inspired dish: a potato casserole that can use either smoked turkey or ham.

Lemon Garlic Roasted Cornish Hen

Moderate

One Cornish hen makes a nice meal for two. In this lemon and garlic-scented version, it roasts to a golden brown before being served up with the flavorful pan juices. Herbed Rice (p. 167) is the optimal accompaniment to this, although roasted or mashed potatoes work nicely, too.

INGREDIENTS

1 Cornish hen, about 4 pounds

1 tablespoon butter

1 tablespoon olive oil

1 lemon

1 teaspoon Herbes de Provence

Fresh cracked pepper and sea salt

2 small cloves garlic or 1 large

Paprika

DIRECTIONS

1. Remove the giblets and neck from the hen and rinse it under cold running water. Drain well.

2. Melt the butter with the olive oil in a small roasting pan; stir in the juice of ½ the lemon and the herbs.

3. Season the inside of the hen with salt and pepper. Coat it on all sides with the melted butter mixture and place it breast side up in the pan.

4. Stuff it with the remaining half lemon, which has been halved again, and the peeled garlic. Season the outside of the hen with more salt and pepper and a sprinkle of paprika.

5. Roast at 350°F for 1 hour 15 minutes, basting every 15–20. When done it will be evenly browned and the thigh will move easily in its joint. Allow to rest for 5–10 minutes, removing the garlic and lemon from the body cavity before serving. Cut in half and serve with Herbed Rice and the pan drippings.

The butter, oil, and lemon juice add about 220 calories to those of the Cornish hen. On the label the brand of hen I use lists 220 calories per 4 ounces; I would "guesstimate" this would be about half a hen, as so much of the little birds seem to consist of bones. If that is the case, each serving of hen with pan drippings would be about 330 calories before adding the rice.

Creamy Scalloped Potatoes with Smoked Turkey
Moderate

Tender slices of potato paired with smoked turkey or ham in creamy sauce make for an elegant casserole supper. Add a salad of greens and winter fruit such as apples or pears with berry vinaigrette to complement the flavors.

INGREDIENTS

2 cups thinly sliced potatoes (about 2 medium potatoes)

4 ounces sliced smoked turkey or ham, cut in 1" x 2" strips

1 tablespoon butter

2 teaspoons flour

¼ teaspoon salt

Few grinds of black pepper

¼ teaspoon Herbes de Provence

¾ cup milk

2 ounces cream cheese

1 ounce shredded Gruyère or other favorite cheese

DIRECTIONS

1. Preheat the oven to 350°F. Place half of the potatoes in a buttered 4" x 6" baking pan. Layer the ham or turkey over the potatoes and the remaining potatoes over the meat.

2. In a small saucepan, melt the butter over low heat. Stir in the flour, salt, pepper, and herbs. Whisk in the milk, increase the heat to medium high, and cook, whisking constantly, until it bubbles and thickens.

3. Remove from heat and whisk in the cream cheese until the cream cheese is melted and the sauce is smooth. Pour over the potatoes and meat.

4. Bake at 350°F for about 45 minutes, until the potatoes are fork tender. Sprinkle with the cheese for the last 5–10 minutes, baking until the cheese melts and bubbles. This makes two generous servings or four modest ones.

Made with smoked turkey the total calorie count is approximately 930; 435 for 2 servings or 220 for 4 moderate servings.

PORK & HAM

It's easy enough to cook a couple pork chop when you're in the mood, but occasionally it's nice to move on to something a little more complex. In addition to the three pork recipes here, there is also a casserole in which you may use either ham or smoked turkey (listed with the poultry entrées) and a variation on macaroni and cheese with bacon and tomato. Other pork-based dishes include a number of Bountiful Breakfasts recipes, as well as Baked Easter Mini Ham (p. 244), Croque Monsieur or Madame (p. 259), and Ginger Honey Pork Roast with Glazed Onions (p. 281).

Bacon and Tomato Mac & Cheese
Moderate

Bacon and tomato buddy up with macaroni and cheese to produce an especially flavorful and hearty dish. This makes two hearty servings. If you don't finish it all, it makes great leftovers!

INGREDIENTS

¾ cup elbow or other preferred macaroni

2 slices bacon, diced

1 tablespoon flour

½ teaspoon instant minced onion

⅜ teaspoon salt, divided

Few grinds pepper

2–3 dashes Tabasco sauce

¾ cup milk

¾ cup shredded cheddar cheese

1 medium tomato, cut in 4 slices

4 teaspoons breadcrumbs

¼ teaspoon mixed Italian herbs or oregano

4 teaspoons grated Parmesan or Romano cheese

1½ teaspoons olive oil

DIRECTIONS

1. Cook the pasta according to package directions until done al dente (tender but not mushy).

2. Fry the bacon in a large heavy saucepan until it is crispy and golden. Stir in the flour, onion, ¼ teaspoon salt, a few grinds of pepper, and 2–3 dashes of Tabasco sauce, cooking and stirring until the flour is integrated.

3. Stir in the milk and cook, stirring up the brown bits from the bottom of the pan, until it is thick and bubbly. Turn off the heat and stir in the cheddar cheese until melted.

4. Stir in the drained, cooked pasta and turn into a lightly oiled 2 cup casserole dish or 4" x 8" baking dish. Combine the breadcrumbs, Italian herbs, ⅛ teaspoon salt, Parmesan or Romano cheese, and olive oil.

5. Arrange the sliced tomato on top of the macaroni and cheese and sprinkle evenly with the herbed breadcrumb mixture.

6. Bake in a preheated 375°F oven for 25–30 minutes, until the breadcrumbs are golden and everything is nice and bubbly. This is great served with steamed spinach or zucchini.

Calories will vary slightly depending on the type of cheese you use. Reduced fat cheddar will produce a casserole with 800 calories total; 200–400 per serving, while sharp cheddar will add 140 calories to that total, making each serving about 245–490 calories per person. If you're feeling adventurous, you can even try mixing together different types of cheese, although you're on your own for that calorie count!

Cuban Roast Pork with Black Beans and Rice

Moderate-Complex

When constructing a somewhat more challenging recipe, it's sometimes nice to enjoy the fruits of your labor for more than one meal. This slightly larger cut of meat will provide generous servings with some of the flavorful meat left over for Cuban Pork Sandwiches (p. 89) if you wish.

INGREDIENTS

SAUCE/MARINADE:

1 lime, squeezed to equal about 3 tablespoons lime juice

Orange juice added to lime juice to equal ¾ cup total

¾ teaspoon ground cumin

¾ teaspoon oregano

1 teaspoon salt

¼ teaspoon pepper

1 large or 2 smaller cloves garlic, minced

MEAT:

1½ pounds boneless center cut pork roast

1 medium onion

DIRECTIONS

1. Combine all the marinade ingredients in a small bowl.

2. Pierce the pork on all sides with a sharp knife and place in a re-sealable plastic bag (1 gallon size works well). If need be, you can use a glass or plastic container, although the bag works best for even coverage.

3. Pour the sauce over the pork and refrigerate at least 12 or up to 24 hours, turning occasionally.

4. About an hour and a half before serving time, place the pork and sliced onion in a small roasting pan. Pour about half the marinade over all, reserving the rest, and roast in a 350°F oven for 45 minutes. Increase the heat to 425°F, pour the remaining marinade over the pork and onion, and roast for an additional 20 or so minutes, until the sauce is mostly reduced and the pork begins to brown.

5. Allow it to rest for 10 minutes before slicing. Serve with Black Beans and Rice and a vegetable of choice. (Roasted summer or winter squash go especially nicely with this; simply toss with a little oil, salt, and pepper and roast for the last 20–30 minutes with the pork.)

The pork and onions will amount to about 270 calories per 4-ounce serving.

(continued)

Black Beans and Rice

INGREDIENTS

2 tablespoons olive oil

½ cup diced onion

¼ cup diced cubanelle or bell peppers

1 large or 2 smaller cloves garlic, peeled and minced

15.5-ounce can reduced sodium black beans

¼ cup orange juice

1 tablespoon red wine vinegar

¼ teaspoon salt, or to taste

½ cup white rice

1¼ cups water

1 teaspoon butter

DIRECTIONS

1. Heat the olive oil in a cast-iron skillet over medium heat. Add the onions, peppers, and garlic and sauté for a couple of minutes, until they are softened but not too brown.

2. Pour in the beans and continue to cook, stirring occasionally, for about 5 minutes. Add in the orange juice, red wine vinegar, and salt, tasting for seasoning. This can be served immediately, but tastes even better if allowed to mellow for a little while; perhaps while the rice cooks and the pork finishes roasting.

3. Combine the rice, water, and butter in a small saucepan with a tight fitting lid. Bring to a boil, reduce heat, and simmer, covered, for about 5 minutes. Turn off the heat and allow the tightly covered rice to continue cooking on retained heat another 15 minutes. Fluff and serve with the beans and pork.

The beans total 640 calories, 215 per 3 servings or 160 per 4 servings;
and 80 calories per ½ cup of cooked rice.

Peachy Pork Chops

Easy

If you wish to prepare only one chop in this manner, simply substitute a 4-ounce individual serving cup of diced peaches in juice for the can of sliced peaches and halve the other ingredients. These pork chops go especially well with either Creamy Mashed Potatoes (p. 165) or Herbed Rice (p. 167) and a green vegetable of choice.

INGREDIENTS

2 bone-in center cut pork chops, 6–8 ounces each

1 tablespoon unsalted butter or 2 teaspoons oil

Freshly ground salt and pepper

8.25-ounce can of sliced peaches in juice

⅛ teaspoon cinnamon

Small pinch of salt

Dash of cloves

1 teaspoon cider vinegar

1 teaspoon cornstarch

1 tablespoon maple syrup or packed brown sugar

DIRECTIONS

1. Place a heavy frying pan over medium high heat. Sauté the pork chops in the butter or oil until nicely browned on one side; about 10 minutes.

2. Season with salt and pepper; turn the pork chops, reduce heat to medium, and continue cooking until browned on both sides and the meat no longer shows pink when the chop is cut into near the bone; about another 10 minutes.

3. While the pork chops are cooking, combine all the remaining ingredients in a small saucepan. Stir to dissolve the cornstarch and then heat to boiling, stirring frequently. Reduce the heat and allow it to simmer for 2–3 minutes to blend flavors; remove from heat.

4. To serve, plate the pork chops and either serve the peach sauce over them or in a separate bowl to spoon over as you wish.

Each 6 ounces of lean pork will equal about 400 calories including the butter or oil; the sauce is 160 total or about 80 calories per serving.

Baked Stuffed Pork Chops

Moderate

Using thin boneless pork chops for this classic comfort entrée ensures even cooking as well as ease of preparation. Removing the chops promptly once done prevents reabsorption of the bacon fat, which cooks off nicely during the baking process. Calories in the bread stuffing will vary; I used an intermediate estimate of 80 calories (per serving) for the bread when calculating the total.

INGREDIENTS

Toasted bread to equal 1½ cups torn pieces, not packed

1 teaspoon instant minced onion

½ teaspoon poultry seasoning, or to taste

6 tablespoons milk

4 slices bacon

4 thin boneless center cut pork chops (8 ounces total)

Salt and pepper

DIRECTIONS

1. Combine the bread, onion, poultry seasoning, and milk, stirring to blend well. Allow the bread to absorb the milk for a minute or two.

2. Meanwhile, lightly oil a baking pan or spray with non-stick cooking spray. Cross one strip of bacon over another at a right angle in the pan. Repeat with the other two pieces of bacon, leaving a little space on the pan between the two bacon crosses. Place one pork chop on each bacon cross and season with salt and pepper.

3. Carefully mound the bread filling onto each pork chop, pressing lightly to make an even layer covering the entire surface. Add a second pork chop on top of each, again seasoning with salt and pepper to taste.

4. Fold the bacon up and over, starting with the strip running the long way of the chops. Then fold the strip running the shorter way, bringing it up and over and tucking in the ends to make a neat packet.

5. Bake at 375°F for a little over an hour, until the bacon is golden and crispy and the pork cooked through. Carefully remove the stuffed pork chops to your serving plate and enjoy. Bake some potatoes along with them for a nice accompaniment, or if you have the oven facilities, try Sweet Potato Oven Fries (p. 269) for a tasty change.

There are about 400 calories per serving of stuffed pork chops.

SEAFOOD & FISH DISHES

There is a bit of fresh fish and seafood to enjoy here, but also a few flavorful creations that begin with canned. Those petite containers of ocean goodness are quite handy for creating properly proportioned seafood dinners for one or two. A couple of other fish dishes to enjoy include Tuna Macaroni Salad in Veggie Shells (p. 86) and Baked Stuffed Shrimp (p. 235).

Linguine with White Clam Sauce
Easy

Fresh hot pasta topped with garlicky clam sauce is one of my favorite ways to enjoy seafood, and this dish is pretty much as easy to make as opening a can of clams. A dash of lemon juice brightens and enhances the flavor of the clam sauce.

INGREDIENTS

1 tablespoon butter

1 tablespoon olive oil

1 small clove garlic, minced, or ¼ teaspoon garlic powder

Small pinch red pepper flakes

6-ounce can of clams

1 teaspoon lemon juice

1 tablespoon parsley flakes

Diced tomatoes and Parmesan cheese for topping, optional

2 servings cooked linguine

DIRECTIONS

1. Heat the butter and olive oil in a small heavy skillet until the butter melts. Add in the garlic and red pepper flakes and sauté a minute or two, until the garlic softens but doesn't brown.

2. Add the clams and their liquid, the lemon juice, and parsley flakes. Bring to a boil, lower the heat, and simmer for about 2–3 minutes to blend the flavors.

3. Pour over the hot cooked linguine, top with diced tomatoes and grated Parmesan cheese, and enjoy.

There are about 310 calories total in the clam sauce alone; 155 each in 2 servings. Check the linguine box for calories in each serving of cooked pasta.

Salmon Patties with Cucumber Cream Sauce

Easy-Moderate

Use a can of wild caught red salmon for optimal flavor and nutritive value in this dish. Combined with a few other simple ingredients, it fries up into flavorful patties that are then topped off with creamy cucumber sauce. Prepare the Cucumber Cream Sauce ahead of time and refrigerate until you're ready to serve the salmon.

INGREDIENTS

7.5-ounce can of red salmon, drained and flaked

1 egg, slightly beaten

¼ cup finely diced onion or 1 tablespoon instant minced

1 teaspoon parsley flakes

1 tablespoon lemon juice

Dash Tabasco sauce

¼ cup fine dry breadcrumbs

2 tablespoons corn oil

Cucumber Cream Sauce (p. 155)

DIRECTIONS

1. Combine the drained, flaked salmon with the egg, onion, parsley flakes, lemon juice, Tabasco sauce, and breadcrumbs. Stir with a fork until everything is well mixed.

2. Heat the oil in a heavy skillet over medium heat. Form the salmon mixture into 6 small patties and fry them in the hot oil, turning once, until they are golden brown and slightly crispy on both sides; about 6–8 minutes.

3. Serve the salmon patties hot, topped with Cucumber Cream Sauce.

There are about 720 calories in the batch of patties (without sauce); 360 in each serving.

(continued)

Cucumber Cream Sauce

INGREDIENTS

½ cup peeled shredded cucumber, drained if necessary*

2 tablespoons mayonnaise

2 tablespoons sour cream

¼ teaspoon salt

2 teaspoons lemon juice

¼ teaspoon dried dill weed or 1 teaspoon fresh

I've made this sauce without any problem using young, fresh cucumbers from my garden. However, if the cucumber you're using is larger or has been sitting around at the store for a while, you may discover it produces quite a bit of excess moisture once you shred it. If this is the case, you'll want to squeeze out some of the liquid before adding it to the sauce; otherwise, it might make everything a bit too runny to properly enjoy.

DIRECTIONS

1. Combine all ingredients and refrigerate sauce.

2. Serve sauce chilled over the hot salmon patties.

Each batch of sauce contains about 250 calories total, or 125 calories divided between two.

Prosciutto-Wrapped Scallops with Lemon Caper Sauce

Easy-Moderate

Large, creamy sea scallops are what you want for this dish. When wrapped in prosciutto and sautéed until golden, the sweet flesh of the scallops almost caramelizes. Rich yet tangy sauce composed of butter, lemon juice, and capers tops things off.

INGREDIENTS

8 ounces sea scallops (about 6 scallops)

Fresh ground salt and pepper

1½ ounces prosciutto (3 thin strips)

1 tablespoon olive oil

1 tablespoon unsalted butter

2 teaspoons lemon juice

1 teaspoon drained capers

DIRECTIONS

1. Season each scallop with salt and pepper. Halve the prosciutto lengthwise and wrap each scallop with one strip.

2. Heat the olive oil in a small heavy skillet over medium high heat. Add the prosciutto-wrapped scallops to the hot pan and sauté, turning once or twice, until each side is golden and the scallops opaque and cooked through; about 5–6 minutes. Remove the scallops to a serving plate.

3. Turn the heat off and immediately swirl the butter, lemon juice, and capers into the hot pan. Pour over the scallops and serve at once. This dish is equally nice accompanied by either Herbed Rice (p. 167) or Creamy Mashed Potatoes (p. 165).

Each serving contains approximately 265 calories.

White Seafood Lasagna

Complex

Here is a seafood lover's variation on the classic Italian dish. Canned crabmeat and shrimp blend with béchamel sauce enriched with cream cheese, enrobing a filling of herbed ricotta and garlic sautéed spinach. A sprinkling of mozzarella tops this ocean inspired indulgence. The lasagna noodles are cooked and then cut to just fit into a 4" x 6" Pyrex baking pan.

INGREDIENTS

1 tablespoon butter

1 tablespoon flour

⅜ teaspoon salt, divided

1/16 teaspoon white pepper

⅛ teaspoon nutmeg

¾ cup milk

1 ounce cream cheese

6-ounce can of tiny shrimp, drained

6-ounce can of crabmeat, drained

3 teaspoons lemon juice, divided

1 tablespoon snipped fresh chives

4 tablespoons grated Parmesan cheese, divided

2 teaspoons olive oil

1 teaspoon minced fresh garlic or ⅛ teaspoon garlic powder

5 ounces fresh spinach

¾ cup low fat ricotta cheese

½ egg (about 2 tablespoons)

½ teaspoon mixed Italian herbs

2 lasagna noodles, cooked al dente in boiling salted water and cut in half crosswise

¾ cup reduced fat mozzarella cheese

DIRECTIONS

1. Make the béchamel by melting the butter in a small saucepan. Stir in the flour, ¼ teaspoon salt, white pepper, and nutmeg.

2. Add the milk all at once, whisking smooth, and continue to whisk until the mixture thickens and bubbles. Remove from the heat and whisk in the cream cheese until the sauce is smooth.

3. Add the drained shrimp and crabmeat, 2 teaspoons of lemon juice, the chives, and 2 tablespoons of Parmesan cheese; set aside.

4. Pour the olive oil into a heavy skillet or frying pan and add the fresh minced garlic, cooking it a minute or two over medium heat just to soften it. Add the spinach and ⅛ teaspoon salt; this would also be the time to add the garlic powder, if you're using that rather than fresh garlic.

(continued)

5. Stir and sauté the spinach for 2–3 minutes, until it is wilted and dark green but not browned. Stir in 1 teaspoon of lemon juice and set aside.

6. Combine the ricotta, egg, mixed herbs, and remaining 2 tablespoons of Parmesan in a small bowl, mixing to combine well.

7. It's now time to construct your lasagna. Preheat the oven to 350°F. Pour about ¾ cup of the seafood sauce into the bottom of the baking pan, covering the bottom entirely. Place two of the half strips of lasagna lengthwise in the pan; they should just fit.

8. Arrange the spinach evenly over the noodles and then drop small spoonfuls of the ricotta filling over the spinach, making it as even as possible. Place the remaining two strips of lasagna on top of the filling, and pour the remaining seafood sauce evenly over all.

9. Place the pan on top of a slightly larger baking pan to catch any extra sauce that might bubble over during the baking process. Bake for 30 minutes; sprinkle evenly with the shredded mozzarella and bake another 30 minutes, until the cheese is lightly browned and the filling cooked through. Allow the lasagna to rest for about 15 minutes before cutting for best results.

The calories in White Seafood Lasagna total 1470; 735 per 2 generous servings, 490 per 3 servings, or 370 per 4 servings.

Fillet of Fish Veronique

Although sole is the traditional fish used in Veronique dishes, any firm, white-fleshed fish will work nicely. Tarragon is the herb of choice, but again, if you don't have an extensive herb and spice cupboard, a bit of Herbes de Provence is a good substitute. The key to poaching fish is to gently cook it without boiling it, and only until it flakes; if overcooked, it may fall apart. Herbed Rice (p. 167) makes a nice accompaniment.

INGREDIENTS

¼ cup white wine

½ cup water

1 teaspoon lemon juice

½ teaspoon instant minced onion

Dash of white pepper

⅛ teaspoon tarragon or Herbes de Provence

8-ounce fillet firm white fish, halved

1 tablespoon butter

2 teaspoons flour

Dash salt

2 tablespoons cream

½ cup seedless green grapes

DIRECTIONS

1. Combine the wine, water, lemon juice, onion, white pepper, and tarragon or herbs in a small skillet or saucepan. Bring to boiling, reduce heat, and add the fish fillets. Allow the fish to poach, the water simmering but not boiling, for about 3–5 minutes, until the flesh turns uniformly opaque. Using a slotted spoon or spatula, carefully remove the fish to a warm serving plate.

2. Bring the poaching liquid back to boiling to reduce it just slightly. Meanwhile, melt the butter, add in the flour and a dash of salt, cooking and stirring for a minute to cook slightly but not brown the flour.

3. Whisk in the hot poaching liquid all at once, cooking and stirring until slightly thickened. Add in the cream and grapes and heat through. Pour over the poached fish and serve at once.

Calories in the sauce and grapes are 330. If prepared with sole add 160 for a total of 490 calories or 245 per serving; with haddock add 200 calories for a total of 530 calories or 265 per serving.

VEGETABLE & VEGETARIAN ENTRÉES & SIDE DISHES

Other side dishes that are listed as part of an entrée recipe include Black Beans and Rice (p. 147) and Coconut Rice (p. 132). Festive Feasts also contains several other vegetable side dishes, including Twice-Baked Cheddar Potatoes (p. 225), Grilled Artichoke with Lemon Basil Aioli (p. 236), Individual Pommes Anna (p. 245), Sweet Potato Oven Fries (p. 269), Coconut Pecan Twice-Baked Sweet Potatoes (p. 274), and Green Beans and Mushrooms with Crispy Shallots (p. 275).

Broccoli Mac & Cheese
Easy-Moderate

Two favorite foods to have with cheese sauce are broccoli and hot pasta. Here they are combined into one flavorful vegetarian entrée that won't leave you hungry. There may even be enough for leftovers (if you're lucky . . .).

INGREDIENTS

½ teaspoon salt, divided

½ cup elbow macaroni

1 cup broccoli florets

1 tablespoon butter

1 tablespoon flour

1 teaspoon Dijon mustard

Dash grated nutmeg

A few grinds black pepper

¾ cup milk

¾ cup grated sharp cheddar cheese

Paprika

DIRECTIONS

1. Bring 2 cups water and ¼ teaspoon salt to a boil in a small saucepan. Add the macaroni, bring back to a boil, and cook for 5 minutes. Add the broccoli florets and boil 2 minutes longer. Drain the macaroni and broccoli; set aside.

2. Meanwhile, melt the butter over low heat in the small saucepan. Add the flour, mustard, ¼ teaspoon salt, nutmeg, and pepper. Whisk in the milk; increase the heat to medium high and bring to a boil, whisking constantly.

3. Add ½ cup of the cheese, whisking until just melted. Remove from the heat and stir in the cooked macaroni and broccoli. Pour into a small buttered casserole dish. Sprinkle with the remaining cheese and a bit of paprika.

4. Bake at 350°F for about ½ hour, until lightly browned and bubbly.

There are 840 calories in all; 420 each in 2 servings.

Corn Pudding

Moderate

This variation on corn pudding utilizes both whole kernel corn and cornmeal. It's easy to make year round; you can use kernels cut from one ear of cooked corn on the cob or substitute frozen thawed or canned drained whole kernel corn. It will make 2 generous servings of corn pudding, or 4 smaller side servings. Try it as the centerpiece of a vegetarian dinner, or pair it with ham, sausage, or chicken and a bright orange vegetable such as winter squash or sweet potatoes.

INGREDIENTS

½ egg, beaten (about 2 tablespoons)

1 tablespoon butter, melted

2 tablespoons sour cream

1 tablespoon cornmeal

¼ cup milk

¼ teaspoon salt

2 teaspoons sugar

¾ cup whole kernel or fresh cut corn

Paprika

DIRECTIONS

1. Combine the egg, butter, sour cream, cornmeal, milk, salt, and sugar in a small bowl, whisking until smooth. Stir in the corn and pour into a small buttered casserole or baking dish. Sprinkle lightly with paprika.

2. Bake for about 30 minutes at 375°F, until the top is puffy and lightly browned. Serve hot.

There are about 420 calories total: 210 each in 2 servings or 105 each in 4.

Creamy Mashed Potatoes

Easy-Moderate

Nothing beats creamy, homemade mashed potatoes, the perfect accompaniment to so many dishes. Use russet or russet type potatoes for the best flavor and texture in this recipe.

INGREDIENTS

1½ cups peeled and cubed russet potatoes

1 cup water

½ teaspoon salt

2 tablespoons half-and-half

1 tablespoon butter

Salt and pepper

DIRECTIONS

1. Place the potatoes, water, and salt in a small saucepan with a tight fitting lid. Bring to a boil, reduce heat to medium low, and slowly boil until the potatoes are tender and the liquid is mostly absorbed, about 15–20 minutes.

2. Drain the potatoes very well. Add in the half-and-half and the butter and mash or whip until they are smooth and fluffy.

3. Season the potatoes to taste with freshly ground salt and pepper and serve at once.

This makes two servings with about 160 calories in each.

Herbed Rice

Easy

Herbed Rice is one of those easy-to-prepare yet delicious sides that goes well with a variety of meat and poultry entrées. Feel free to vary the broth used depending on what the rice will accompany; although the chicken broth gives this dish its classic flavor, either beef or vegetable broth can be used instead.

INGREDIENTS

½ cup jasmine rice

4 teaspoons butter

1 teaspoon Herbes de Provence or parsley

1 teaspoon instant minced onion

¼ teaspoon salt

1 cup chicken or vegetable broth

DIRECTIONS

1. In a medium saucepan, sauté the rice in the butter until it changes color but does not brown.

2. Add the herbs, onion, salt, and broth and bring to a boil. Lower the heat and simmer, covered, for 5 minutes. Turn off the heat and allow the rice to stand, covered, for another 15 minutes.

3. Fluff the rice and serve.

There are about 470 calories in all, or 285 per serving. Although this is the serving size listed on the rice package, I seldom eat this much rice in one sitting, so you may just have some leftovers (and fewer calories consumed!).

Potato Salad
Moderate

This makes a modest amount of potato salad for two people (about ½ cup each). It's very easy to double or triple the recipe, should you wish to.

INGREDIENTS

1 medium potato, preferably red skinned (about 1 cup diced cooked)

Salt and pepper to taste

1 teaspoon snipped chives or ½ teaspoon instant minced onion

½ teaspoon fresh or ¼ teaspoon dried dill weed

1 teaspoon fresh or ½ teaspoon dried parsley flakes

5 pimento stuffed olives, sliced, or 2 tablespoons diced pickles

1 tablespoon sour cream

1 tablespoon mayonnaise

DIRECTIONS

1. Boil the unpeeled potato in salted water until just tender. Drain and allow it to cool thoroughly; overnight in the fridge is fine. If using red or other thin skinned potatoes, leave the skin on; otherwise peel if you prefer.

2. Dice the potato coarsely and place in a good-sized salad bowl or small mixing bowl. Add all the remaining ingredients.

3. Serve immediately or refrigerate, covered, until ready to eat. This makes one cup of potato salad.

There are 250 calories in all, or 125 per ½ cup serving.

Tian for Two
Moderate-Complex

Tian is a layered casserole of garden fresh vegetables that looks as delectable as it tastes. It may be served as a hearty side dish, but is also perfectly acceptable as the main course for a light summer supper. Fresh herbs and seasonal vegetables make the flavors in this dish with Provençal roots really shine.

INGREDIENTS

1 small onion, thinly sliced

1 medium clove garlic, minced

3 teaspoons olive oil, divided

1 cup peeled, thinly sliced eggplant

1 medium russet or red skinned potato, thinly sliced

1 small zucchini or summer squash 6"–8", thinly sliced, about a cup

1 large tomato, thinly sliced

Freshly ground sea salt and black pepper

A few leaves of fresh basil, stem removed, rolled and cut thin

A small sprig fresh rosemary and/or thyme, minced or crumbled

1 tablespoon butter

¼ cup shredded or shaved Parmesan cheese

DIRECTIONS

1. Butter a 3-cup casserole dish or 4" x 6" baking pan well. Sauté the onion, and garlic lightly in 1 teaspoon of the oil; set aside. Sauté the eggplant slices in the remaining 2 teaspoons of olive oil; set aside.

2. In the casserole dish or baking pan, layer in order the potatoes, onions, and garlic, eggplant, zucchini, and tomato, sprinkling each layer with some of the salt, pepper, and herbs.

3. Dot the top evenly with the butter and bake at 375°F for about 35–40 minutes. Sprinkle the cheese over the top once the vegetables test fork tender and bake another 5 minutes, until it just melts and bubbles. Serve hot or at room temperature.

There are about 540 calories in the entire Tian, or 270 per serving.

DELECTABLE DESSERTS

We probably each have a favorite dessert or two—whether pudding, cake, pie, or cookies—and this section includes some of each. Because in some cases we're again dealing with very small measurements, this is an area where your small batch measuring tools, such as a converted medicine dropper or mini measure, come in especially handy. Review the egg dividing techniques described in both the Welcome and Bountiful Breakfasts sections if you need to, and get out your smaller sized baking tins and cookie sheet. (Also keep in mind that I've formulated the various recipes using skim milk when milk is called for.)

PUDDING TIME

This quartet of puddings definitely doesn't come from a box. Ranging from easy to complex, each is unique and delicious . . . and amazingly, not one of them is chocolate! A fifth delectable dessert, Blueberries in a Cloud, combines fresh berry cream filling with delicate meringue shells. Enjoy!

Ricotta Pudding

Easy

Ricotta Pudding is a snap to prepare and makes a refreshing, not-too-sweet dessert. Enjoy it on a hot summer's day when you don't want to use the stove, or as an anytime ending to your favorite Italian feast. The freshly made pudding may also be placed in foil reinforced cupcake pan liners and frozen; simply peel away the liner to enjoy. Fiori di Sicilia is a vanilla-citrus flavoring available through King Arthur Flour. I use it in a variety of recipes, although if you don't have access to it, a bit of vanilla and orange extract or zest will do just fine instead.

INGREDIENTS

2 tablespoons finely diced dried apricots

1 tablespoon orange juice

¼ cup heavy cream

3 tablespoons confectioner's sugar

6 tablespoons part-skim ricotta

Dash cinnamon, optional

3 drops Fiori di Sicilia or ¼ teaspoon vanilla extract and ⅛ teaspoon orange extract/grated zest

2 tablespoons finely chopped or grated semi-sweet chocolate

DIRECTIONS

1. Place the diced apricots and the orange juice in a small bowl and allow them to macerate while preparing the rest of the pudding.

2. Whip together the cream and confectioner's sugar until the mixture forms soft peaks. Fold in the ricotta, the apricot/orange juice mixture, the cinnamon, and the vanilla/orange flavorings.

3. You may either serve at once or cover and refrigerate for up to a couple of days. Just before serving, divide between 2 dishes, sprinkle with the grated chocolate, and serve. If you choose to freeze your Ricotta Pudding, top with the chocolate after filling the cupcake wrappers and before popping in the freezer.

There are about 580 calories total in this recipe, or 290 per serving.

Sticky Date Pudding with Toffee Sauce

Complex

Here is an indulgent comfort food pudding just right to enjoy during the colder months of fall and winter. Medjool dates are a particularly large and flavorful variety frequently available to buy by the pound (or ounce!). If you can't find medjool dates, substitute whatever variety is readily available; just be sure to use actual diced dates, not the date pieces that often contain fillers; they would change the flavor and texture of the pudding, and not for the better. Serve your pudding with a scoop of vanilla ice cream and a drizzle of warm Toffee Sauce. This recipe makes enough for four servings, because you're going to want leftovers!

INGREDIENTS

6 medjool dates, coarse diced to equal ½ cup

½ teaspoon fresh grated ginger root or ¼ teaspoon powdered ginger

½ cup water

¼ cup orange juice

½ teaspoon baking soda

3 tablespoons butter

⅓ cup sugar

½ teaspoon vanilla extract

1 egg

½ cup plus 2 tablespoons flour

¼ teaspoon baking powder

⅛ teaspoon salt

DIRECTIONS

1. Combine the dates, ginger, water, and orange juice in a small heavy saucepan. Bring to a boil, reduce heat, and simmer for about 1 minute. Remove from the heat and stir in the baking soda, which will foam up as you do so.

2. Allow the date mixture to sit for about 20 minutes, until it has cooled to lukewarm.

3. Meanwhile, butter and flour a 4" x 6" baking pan (3-cup Pyrex pan). Cream together the butter, sugar, and vanilla until the mixture is light and fluffy. Beat in the egg and then beat in the combined flour, salt, and baking powder; the dough will be fairly stiff. On low speed, beat in the cooled dates and liquid until everything is just mixed together.

4. Pour into the prepared pan and bake in a preheated 350° oven for approximately 30 minutes, until the top is shiny and slightly firm to touch. Serve warm or at room temperature topped with warm Toffee Sauce and vanilla ice cream.

There are about 1230 calories in the pudding cake base; 310 per serving before adding sauce and ice cream.

(continued)

Toffee Sauce

INGREDIENTS

½ cup dark brown sugar

1 tablespoon corn syrup or honey

¼ cup butter

¼ cup plus 2 tablespoons cream

½ teaspoon vanilla extract

DIRECTIONS

1. Combine all ingredients in a small heavy saucepan and bring to a full boil over medium-high heat. Reduce the heat and boil for one minute. Stir in the vanilla. Serve warm over Sticky Date Pudding.

Total calories for the sauce are about 1120, or about 280 per serving.

Strawberry Bread & Butter Pudding
Easy

Based on an old English recipe, Strawberry Bread & Butter Pudding is a breeze to prepare in hot summer weather. The sweet and juicy berries soak into the soft white bread to make a tempting crimson pudding. Although lightly buttering the bread may seem odd, the flavor it produces helps make the hallmark flavor of this unique dessert.

INGREDIENTS

1½ cups rinsed, hulled, halved, or quartered strawberries

2–4 tablespoons sugar, depending on sweetness of berries and personal taste

2 teaspoons orange liqueur or orange juice

4 slices soft white bread

Softened or whipped butter

Sweetened whipped cream

Fresh berries and mint leaves for garnish, optional

DIRECTIONS

1. Use a large custard cup for each serving. If preparing for 2 or more, you may use a small casserole dish or mixing bowl instead.

2. Crush the strawberries well, using a pastry cutter or fork. Stir in the sugar and liqueur or orange juice and allow them to macerate for about 5 minutes.

3. Meanwhile, lightly butter the bread on one side only. Remove the crusts and cut some of the bread to fit in the bottom of the desired dish, buttered side down. Cut more bread to line the sides almost to the top, placing the buttered sides out.

4. Pour in half the berries and cover with another piece of bread. Add the rest of the berries and cover with the remaining bread, butter side up. Cover securely with wax paper or plastic wrap, pushing the bread down evenly into the berry mixture. If you are able to fit a small weight, such as a saucer, on top of the pudding, this will help the bread absorb the berry juices better. If not, don't worry about it; just press the bread down once or twice while the pudding settles.

5. Refrigerate at least four hours; overnight is even better. When you're ready to serve, turn the pudding out onto individual dessert dishes. If using a small casserole dish or bowl, turn onto a serving plate and slice into two servings.

6. Serve topped with sweetened whipped cream, garnished with more fresh berries if you wish, and a mint leaf or two.

Calories per serving without cream are 230; add about 125 more if you include a dollop of freshly whipped sweetened cream.

Citrus Soufflé Pudding Cake

Moderate

This light and lemony pudding cake separates into 2 layers: sponge-like cake topping over a custardy pudding base. It's tasty any time of the year, and especially delicious topped with a dollop of fresh whipped cream.

INGREDIENTS

1 large egg, separated
1 tablespoon butter, melted
½ cup sugar, divided
1 tablespoon lemon juice
1 tablespoon orange juice
½ teaspoon grated lemon zest or ¼ teaspoon pure lemon extract

½ teaspoon grated orange zest or ¼ teaspoon pure orange extract
½ cup water
3 tablespoons flour
¼ teaspoon baking powder
⅛ teaspoon salt

DIRECTIONS

1. Preheat the oven to 350°F. Whisk together until smooth the egg yolk, melted butter, ¼ cup of the sugar, the lemon and orange juices, and zests or flavorings.

2. Combine the flour, baking powder, and salt and whisk into the yolk mixture until smooth. Whisk in the water and set aside.

3. Beat the egg white until frothy. Add the remaining sugar 1 tablespoon at a time, beating to glossy peaks. Pour the citrus egg yolk mixture over the beaten whites and stir together quickly until just well blended.

4. Pour into a 2-cup casserole dish, set it in a 9" cake pan, and carefully add about 1" of very hot water to the cake pan. Bake for about 35 minutes, until the top is light golden brown and springs back when gently touched.

5. Remove from the oven and the pan of water and allow it to cool a few minutes before serving. This is good either warm or chilled. Garnish with fresh berries and lightly sweetened whipped cream if you wish. Refrigerate any leftovers to enjoy within a couple of days.

There are approximately 630 total calories or 315 calories per serving, before adding whipped cream or berries.

Blueberries in a Cloud
Moderate

Blueberries in a Cloud is one of those recipes that doesn't quite fit into a category such as puddings or pies, but rather hovers somewhere in between. Fresh plump blueberries are folded into a whipped cream and cream cheese mixture and piled onto crisp meringue shells. It's a splendid way to end most any meal, and an especially nice way to utilize blueberries when they're at their seasonal best. You can make this dessert slightly less indulgent by using light cream cheese in place of regular as I do; the choice is up to you.

INGREDIENTS

MERINGUE SHELLS
1 egg white

1 teaspoon lime juice or lemon juice

6 tablespoons confectioner's sugar

BLUEBERRY CREAM TOPPING
2 ounces regular or light cream cheese

¼ cup confectioner's sugar

½ teaspoon vanilla extract

½ teaspoon lemon or lime zest

¼ cup heavy cream

½ cup fresh blueberries

Mint leaves and extra blueberries for garnish

DIRECTIONS

1. To make the Meringue Shells, whip the egg white and lemon or lime juice until foamy. Gradually beat in the sugar, a spoonful at a time, until the mixture forms soft glossy peaks.

2. Form into 2 thin circles, about 5"–6" in diameter, on a parchment- or wax paper–lined baking sheet. Give each meringue a slight rim, the better to eventually hold the blueberry cream filling.

3. Bake at 250°F for one hour. Allow the pan of meringues to remain in the oven with the heat turned off and door slightly open for another hour. Carefully remove from the parchment paper to enjoy at once or to wrap airtight for another day.

4. To make the Blueberry Cream Topping, beat together the cream cheese, confectioner's sugar, vanilla, and lemon or lime zest until the mixture is smooth and creamy.

5. Add the heavy cream and beat again until it thickens and again becomes smooth and creamy. Fold in the blueberries and fill the meringue shells just before serving. Garnish with mint leaves and extra blueberries, if desired.

The meringue shells total 200 calories, or 100 per serving, and the filling, made with light cream cheese, is approximately 500 calories total, or 250 per serving, making each finished dessert just about 350 calories.

TIME FOR PIE

We're now heading into the land of pies-proper; four little mini pies just right two servings. They each utilize the same butter-rich pie crust; mix up a batch from the basic recipe and freeze whatever you don't use right away for another day. You will need an individual-sized pie plate for each of these recipes; the same 4" size also used for the mini quiches in the Bountiful Breakfasts portion of the book. They can frequently be found in specialty cookware stores or large grocery stores; if this fails, try checking online.

A Big Fat Peach Mini Pie

Moderate

No more peeling or pitting with this pie; all you need to do is open a can of peaches! Top it off with a dollop of Sweet Almond Whipped Cream and you have a peachy treat that's sure to please.

INGREDIENTS

2 tablespoons sugar

½ teaspoon cornstarch

¼ teaspoon cinnamon

Dash of salt

1 small (8.25-ounce) can sliced peaches in light syrup

½ teaspoon lemon juice

¼ teaspoon almond extract

2 individual portions Pie Crust Dough (p. 184)

Milk and sugar for glazing crust

Slivered almonds, optional

Sweet Almond Whipped Cream

DIRECTIONS

1. Combine the sugar, cornstarch, cinnamon, and salt in a small saucepan. Stir in the peaches in their syrup, lemon juice, and almond extract. Bring to a full boil, stirring so that it won't stick.

2. Cool to room temperature before filling crust; placing the saucepan in a larger pan or bowl of cold water will expedite the process. Roll out each chilled portion of dough on a lightly floured board. Fit one half into your 6" pie tin.

3. Pour in the peach filling; dab a little milk over the bottom crust and filling. Turn the edges under evenly and flute them. Sprinkle the top of the pie with a few slivered almonds, if you wish, and a generous sprinkling of sugar.

4. Bake at 375°F for approximately 35 minutes, until the crust is evenly browned all over. Serve warm or at room temperature; it's especially good with peach or vanilla ice cream or with Sweet Almond Whipped Cream. This makes one very generous serving right out of the pan, or 2 or 4 more moderate. Hint: For easy removal, cut into quarters, placing 1 or 2 on each dessert plate.

There are about 850 calories in the entire pie with a sprinkling of sugar and almonds on the top; 425 for half a pie or 215 for a quarter serving, before adding cream or ice cream.

(continued)

Sweet Almond Whipped Cream

INGREDIENTS

¼ cup chilled heavy cream

1 tablespoon confectioner's sugar

2–3 teaspoons almond liqueur (or use
¼ teaspoon almond extract if you prefer)

DIRECTIONS

1. Combine all the ingredients in a small chilled bowl and beat until soft peaks form.

This makes 2 servings of whipped cream at approximately 130 calories per serving.

Pie Crust Dough
Moderate

You'll see Pie Crust Dough featured in the Bountiful Breakfasts section of this book as well; it's a versatile recipe that divides easily into portions and freezes well. Simply place in sealable plastic bags or wrap in plastic wrap, label, and refrigerate up to a week or freeze for up to 3 months.

INGREDIENTS

1 cup all-purpose flour

½ teaspoon sugar

½ teaspoon salt

½ cup cold butter

½ teaspoon mild vinegar or lemon juice

3 tablespoons cold water

DIRECTIONS

1. Combine the flour, sugar, and salt in a medium-sized mixing bowl.

2. Using a cheese grater, shred the butter into small pieces, or alternatively cut it into the dry ingredients until the mixture resembles coarse crumbs.

3. Combine the vinegar or lemon juice with the water and sprinkle it over the mixture, stirring lightly with a fork until it is all integrated (it may still appear rather crumbly at this point).

4. Gather the dough together with your hands and form into four equal balls. Place in plastic wrap or a plastic storage bag and refrigerate at least half an hour before rolling out for the best results. You may also freeze the dough at this point; when ready to use, remove the amount you need and microwave for just a few seconds at time, until it's thawed enough to roll but still quite cold. Roll out thin on a floured surface and fill your pie plate, leaving a generous overhang for fluting the edges.

There are 1240 calories in the entire recipe; 310 per serving for a single crust or 620 per serving when making a double-crusted pie.

Baby Blueberry Pie
Moderate

Use either fresh or frozen blueberries to make this scrumptious little pie. For easiest serving, cut it into quarters before removing from the pan, especially if you wish to enjoy it hot.

INGREDIENTS

2 cups blueberries
½ cup sugar
1 tablespoon cornstarch
1 teaspoon lemon juice

¼ cup water
2 individual portions Pie Crust Dough
   (p. 184)
Milk and sugar for glazing top

DIRECTIONS

1. Combine the blueberries, sugar, and cornstarch in a medium saucepan. Add the lemon juice and water, stirring to smooth out the cornstarch. Bring to a boil over medium heat, stirring frequently.

2. Cool the filling to room temperature before filling your pie shell. Roll out the crust as directed above, pouring the filling into the pastry-lined pie pan. Brushing a little milk or water around the edges of the lower crust before adding the top will help them adhere to one another.

3. Roll out the top crust, cutting a few slits or other designs to allow steam to escape; fit carefully over the filling and bottom crust. Pinch together the edges, folding under evenly and then either fluting the crust with your fingers or flattening it with a fork or spoon.

4. Brush the top with a little milk and sprinkle with sugar. Bake at 375–400°F for about 25 minutes, until the filling begins to bubble and the crust has browned nicely. This is especially tasty served warm topped with a scoop of vanilla ice cream.

The entire pie has about 1180 calories; 295 per quarter piece or 590 per half.

Fresh Strawberry Pie
Moderate

What better way to enjoy luscious fresh strawberries than in this jewel-like pie? It's as pretty to look at as it is delicious. Because strawberries are naturally low in calories and the recipe only utilizes one crust, it's also a somewhat healthier indulgence than most pies . . . at least before adding whipped cream!

INGREDIENTS

1 individual portion Pie Crust Dough (p. 184)
1¼ cups fresh strawberries
¼ cup cold water
¼ cup sugar

1½ teaspoons lemon juice
2 teaspoons cornstarch
Dash salt

DIRECTIONS

1. Roll the pie crust dough very thin, so that you have a good amount of overlap when placed in an individual pie tin. Make high, fluted edges on the dough, prick it with a fork or sharp knife, and set it aside to rest for about half an hour. Bake in a preheated 400°F oven until light golden brown, about 10–15 minutes. Placing foil or an extra pie plate on top of the unbaked crust and filling with dry rice or beans will help prevent the baking crust from shrinking back into the pan.

2. While the crust is cooling, prepare the filling. Wash the strawberries under cold running water, pat dry with paper towels, and hull. Set aside a cup of the most uniform, perfect berries; in this case, smaller is actually better. Chop the remaining berries and combine in a blender with the water, sugar, and lemon juice. Whirl until the mixture is mostly smooth. Combine in a small saucepan along with the cornstarch and salt, stirring until smooth.

3. Cook over medium heat, whisking constantly, until it thickens and boils. Boil gently for 1 minute, still whisking; remove from the heat, and chill by placing the base of the pan in a larger container of ice cold water.

4. Once it's cool but not cold, place about 2 tablespoons of the glaze mixture into the baked pie shell, smoothing to coat it well. Mound the strawberries into the pie plate and pour the rest of the glaze evenly over the berries, coating them well. Chill for at least 1 hour, until the glaze is set. Top with sweetened whipped cream and enjoy.

This entire little pie is about 580 calories before adding cream; 270 per half or 135 per quarter, which as pies go is not bad at all.

Crumb-Topped Apple Pie

Moderate-Complex

Don't be afraid to mound the apples up high in this apple mini pie; some settling is to be expected. Any firm, tart apple will do; use whatever variety you prefer.

INGREDIENTS

1 individual portion Pie Crust Dough (p. 184)

1 large baking apple, peeled, cored, and
   thinly sliced (2 cups)

2 tablespoons sugar

1 teaspoon flour

Dash salt

¼ teaspoon cinnamon and a pinch nutmeg or
   ¼ teaspoon apple pie spice

CRUMB TOPPING

1 tablespoon butter, melted

2 tablespoons sugar

¼ cup flour

¼ teaspoon cinnamon

DIRECTIONS

1. Roll out the pie crust dough and fit loosely into an individual pie plate.

2. Combine the sliced apple, sugar, flour, salt, and spices and turn into the pastry-lined pan, pressing into a mound shape.

3. Combine all the topping ingredients until the mixture is crumbly and sprinkle carefully over the apple filling, again patting it into place. Bake at 375°F for about 40 minutes, until it is browned and bubbly and the apples feel tender when pierced with a sharp knife or fork.

There are about 840 total calories in this mini pie; 210 per quarter or 420 per half.

CUPCAKES & CAKES

Did you ever really want a cupcake, but didn't want the fuss of making an entire batch of them? If so, the next three recipes are for you. Each makes two cupcakes, and includes a frosting recipe made for two to boot! The cupcake and frosting recipes all taste good in various combinations, so feel free to mix and match them. We then move on to cakes; there are three basic cake recipes included; each intended to be baked in a 6" round cake pan. There are also recipe variations for the Hot Milk Sponge Cake, and a couple of frosting recipes you can use interchangeably on any of the basic cakes. You will note that some of the recipes call for "cake flour"; if you want optimal results in your baking, please invest in a box of it. If cake flour is not specified in the recipe, it's fine to use regular (all-purpose) flour instead.

Two Chocolate Cupcakes

Moderate

The secret to these moist little cupcakes is substituting mayonnaise for the egg and oil or butter you'd normally use. And if you'd like more than twp cupcakes, simply double or triple the ingredients . . . just remember to double or triple your frosting ingredients as well.

INGREDIENTS

¼ cup flour

4 teaspoons dark cocoa powder

⅛ teaspoon baking soda

2 tablespoons plus 2 teaspoons sugar

¼ cup water

4 teaspoons mayonnaise

⅛ teaspoon vanilla extract

Chocolate Whipped Cream

DIRECTIONS

1. Preheat oven to 375°F. Use a large liquid measuring cup or small mixing bowl to combine the flour, cocoa, baking soda, and sugar. Whisk in the combined water, mayonnaise, and vanilla until the batter is smooth.

2. Divide batter between two greased and floured or paper-lined muffin cups. I suggest spritzing the paper liners with a bit of non-stick cooking spray to facilitate easy removal, allowing the spray to overlap some onto the muffins tin's surface as well.

3. Bake for 20–25 minutes, until the tops are rounded and the cupcakes spring back when lightly touched. Cool thoroughly before frosting.

There are about 185 calories per plain cupcake. When frosted with Chocolate Whipped Cream, the total will be 320 calories.

(continued)

Chocolate Whipped Cream

INGREDIENTS

2 tablespoons heavy cream
1 tablespoon confectioner's sugar
1 teaspoon cocoa

DIRECTIONS

1. Combine all ingredients in a small mixing bowl and beat until the cream reaches a frosting consistency.

2. Spread or pipe onto cooled cupcakes.

The calories are 135 per serving for the whipped cream frosting alone.

Applesauce Spice Cupcakes

Moderate

This moist little cupcake doesn't require any eggs either; in this case the applesauce and oil do the trick. Frost with the Caramel Cream Icing and you'll experience the cupcake version of a caramel apple.

INGREDIENTS

¼ cup unsweetened applesauce

3 tablespoons sugar

4 teaspoons oil

¼ teaspoon vanilla extract

¼ teaspoon apple pie spice or combined cinnamon and nutmeg

¼ cup flour

⅛ teaspoon baking soda

Caramel Cream Icing or other topping of choice

DIRECTIONS

1. Preheat oven to 350°F. In a small bowl or large liquid measuring cup, whisk together the applesauce, sugar, oil, and vanilla. Stir in the combined dry ingredients until the batter is smooth.

2. Divide batter between two lined and/or oiled and floured cupcake cups. If using paper liners, spritz them with a bit of non-stick cooking spray; adding a little oil to the surface of the pan itself is also a good idea, as this allows the batter to spread and makes a nice big cupcake.

3. Bake for 25–30 minutes, until the cupcakes are puffed, golden, and springs back when lightly touched. Cool completely before frosting.

There are 225 calories in one plain cupcake. When frosted with Caramel Cream Icing, the total is 445 calories.

(continued)

Caramel Cream Icing

If you don't use the full portion of icing on your cupcakes, use the leftover as sweetener for coffee or other hot drinks, or try combining it with peanut butter or another nut butter for a tasty spread on toast or biscuits.

INGREDIENTS

2 tablespoons sugar

1 tablespoon water

Dash salt

1 tablespoon plus 1 teaspoon half-and-half, more or less

2 tablespoons butter

¼ cup confectioner's sugar or slightly more

DIRECTIONS

1. In a small saucepan, combine the sugar, water, and salt. Bring to a boil and cook, swirling the pan occasionally, until the mixture caramelizes (becomes dark golden brown); watch closely, as it will burn easily near the end of the process.

2. Quickly pour in the half-and-half, stirring until the two liquids are thoroughly combined; be careful, as the hot caramel will bubble up when the cool cream is added. Immediately remove from the heat and allow it to cool, undisturbed, until it reaches room temperature. The sauce should be very thick, but still easy to stir. If it's too thick, add another teaspoon of half-and-half and heat it just to boiling again.

3. Once it has again cooled (this is important for the frosting's texture), using a metal soup spoon, beat in the butter and then the confectioner's sugar, until the icing is smooth and creamy.

This totals about 440 calories of finished icing; 220 in each serving.

Little White Cupcakes
Moderate

Unlike the other single cupcake recipes, Little White Cupcake does require some egg; but egg in such tiny quantities is very difficult to measure. The solution to this quandary is to invest in a container of powdered egg whites, available in the baking section of most stores. Pick it up when purchasing your cake flour, something else you'll require for this recipe. It's an easy investment that will store for a good long time, ready to use when you need it.

INGREDIENTS

2 tablespoons butter, softened

¼ cup sugar

¼ teaspoon vanilla extract

4–6 drops almond flavoring, optional

2 tablespoons milk

¼ cup + 1 tablespoon cake flour

¼ teaspoon baking powder

¾ teaspoon dried egg white

Dash salt

4 teaspoons water

Fresh Strawberry Buttercream

DIRECTIONS

1. Preheat oven to 350°F. Combine the very soft or slightly melted butter, sugar, and flavorings in a small bowl. Beat with a spoon until smooth and creamy.

2. Gradually stir in the milk, again creaming until smooth. Beat in the combined flour, baking powder, dried egg white, and salt. Last, add in the water, again beating until smooth.

3. Divide batter between two prepared cupcake liners (I advise spritzing the liner and cupcake pan with non-stick cooking spray) and bake for about 25 minutes, until puffed and the top springs back when lightly touched with your fingertip. Because this is a white cupcake, it may not show much color on the top even when it's done. Cool before frosting as desired.

One cupcake is approximately 280 calories before frosting; when frosted with Fresh Strawberry Buttercream the calories will total 470.

(continued)

Fresh Strawberry Buttercream

Fresh strawberries add special flavor to this pretty pink frosting. The amount of confectioner's sugar used may vary depending on the juiciness of the strawberry; look for a creamy, fairly stiff consistency, as the berries often continue to produce juice after the frosting is complete.

INGREDIENTS

2 tablespoons butter, softened

1 tablespoon finely diced strawberry

6–8 tablespoons confectioner's sugar

DIRECTIONS

1. Cream together the softened butter and 4 tablespoons of the confectioner's sugar.

2. Add in the strawberries, beating well with a metal or small wooden spoon.

3. Beat in enough additional confectioner's sugar to attain desired consistency.

Each individual batch of frosting is about 440 calories by itself, or 220 per serving.

Hot Milk Sponge Cake

Moderate

Hot Milk Sponge Cake is delicious as is, even better served with fresh fruit or berries and whipped cream. It also forms the base for these other classics: Pineapple Upside-Down Cake (p. 203), Pastel de Tres Leches (p. 246), and Boston Cream Pie (p. 204).

INGREDIENTS

1 egg, separated

½ cup sugar, divided

½ teaspoon vanilla extract

¼ teaspoon pure orange flavoring

¼ cup milk

½ cup cake flour

DIRECTIONS

1. Preheat the oven to 350°F and prepare your 6" baking pan by placing a cut round of wax or parchment paper in the base and coating the base only with non-stick cooking spray or a small amount of cooking oil.

2. Place the egg white in a small high-sided bowl, and place the egg yolk in a slightly larger bowl. Beat the white until foamy.

3. Gradually add 2 tablespoons of the sugar, beating it to soft glossy peaks; set aside.

4. Beat the egg yolk with the flavorings and 4 tablespoons of the sugar until thick and lemon colored.

5. Heat the milk to just under boiling; this can be done either in the microwave or in a small pan on the stovetop. Quickly add the hot milk to the yolk mixture, beating constantly; it will turn nice and foamy.

6. Sift the flour and the remaining 2 tablespoons sugar over this mixture, beating them in until just thoroughly mixed. Immediately fold the beaten egg white in by hand, until just well incorporated.

7. Pour into the prepared pan and bake for approximately 25–30 minutes, until the top is puffed, golden, and springs back when lightly touched. Allow the cake to cool in the pan for 2–3 minutes, run a knife blade around to loosen the edges, and turn out onto a wire rack to cool completely.

Total calories for the plain cake are about 670, or 170 per ¼ serving; 110 per ⅙.

Snowy White Cake
Moderate

This delicate white cake makes one 6" layer (or 6–8 good-sized cupcakes). It's a great treat for a special day—or any day you feel like treating yourself.

INGREDIENTS

¼ cup unsalted butter, softened
½ cup sugar
½ teaspoon pure vanilla extract
¼ teaspoon natural almond flavoring
¾ cup cake flour

1 teaspoon baking powder
¼ teaspoon salt
¼ cup milk
2 egg whites

DIRECTIONS

1. Preheat oven to 350°F. Butter and flour the bottom and sides of your 6" cake pan. I suggest buttering the cake pan rather than spraying it with cooking spray, as the cake does tend to adhere to the pan otherwise.

2. Beat together the butter, sugar, and flavorings until light and fluffy. Add the combined dry ingredients and the milk; beat again until smooth and creamy.

3. Add the egg whites and beat until smooth. Turn into the prepared cake pan.

4. Bake for about 20 minutes, until the surface is light golden brown and springs back when lightly touched. Cool in pan for 5 minutes before turning out to cool completely. Frost with Fluffy White Frosting, or as desired.

There is a total of 1140 calories in this cake; 285 per ¼ serving or 190 per ⅙ serving before frosting.

(continued)

Fluffy White Frosting
Moderate

Fluffy White Frosting forms a billowy cloud of sweet goodness over whatever cake you choose to spread it. It will generously cover a 6" layer or half a dozen cupcakes.

INGREDIENTS

2 tablespoons light corn syrup

¼ cup water

½ cup sugar

Dash salt

1 egg white

1 teaspoon vanilla extract

DIRECTIONS

1. Combine the corn syrup, water, sugar, and salt in a small heavy saucepan. Bring to boiling, using the smaller burner on your stove if you have one, stirring it occasionally to dissolve the sugar.

2. Once the mixture has reached a full boil, allow it to boil for 3 full minutes without stirring; tilt the pan occasionally to facilitate even cooking, if need be.

3. Meanwhile, beat the egg white until it's slightly thickened and foamy. With the beater running on high, pour the boiling hot syrup over the egg white in a thin stream, beating continuously. Beat on high for approximately 2 minutes, until the frosting is thick, creamy, and snowy white.

4. Fold in the vanilla and frost your 6" cake of choice; this will frost it generously.

There are 500 calories in the entire recipe; 125 per ¼ serving or about 95 per ⅙ serving.

Dark Chocolate Cake

Moderate

If you prefer, you can use this recipe to make 6–8 cupcakes rather than the 6" round cake. Reduce the baking time to approximately 20 minutes rather than 30.

INGREDIENTS

½ cup plus 1 tablespoon cake flour or ½ cup
    all-purpose flour

3 tablespoons dark cocoa powder

½ cup sugar

½ teaspoon baking powder

¼ teaspoon baking soda

¼ teaspoon salt

1 egg

¼ cup milk

3 tablespoons corn oil

½ teaspoon vanilla extract

¼ cup water

DIRECTIONS

1. Preheat oven to 350°F. Combine the dry ingredients in a medium mixing bowl; whisk to combine.

2. Add the egg, milk, oil, and vanilla, whisking until smooth. Add the water and whisk again.

3. Pour into a buttered and floured 6" cake pan. Bake for about 30 minutes, until the cake springs back when touched. Cool for 10 minutes before loosening and turning out of the pan.

4. Frost with Chocolate Ganache Buttermilk Frosting, or simply serve with a scoop of your favorite ice cream and drizzle of chocolate sauce.

There are just under 1100 calories in the entire cake;
275 per ¼ serving or 185 per ⅙ before frosting.

{continued}

Chocolate Ganache Buttercream Frosting

This rich and creamy frosting is equally delicious spread over white, yellow, or chocolate cake. I personally find the combination of delicate almond scented white cake and chocolate fudge to be my favorite.

INGREDIENTS

¼ cup heavy cream

1 tablespoon light corn syrup

½ cup good quality semi-sweet chocolate
   chips

2 tablespoons butter

½ teaspoon vanilla extract

1 cup confectioner's sugar

1 tablespoon unsweetened cocoa powder

DIRECTIONS

1. Heat the cream and corn syrup to just under boiling. Remove from heat and stir in the chocolate chips until they are melted.

2. Stir in the butter and vanilla, beating until smooth. Last, add combined confectioner's sugar and cocoa, again beating until smooth. This frosting will thicken as it cools; I recommend chilling it in a larger bowl of cold water.

3. Once it begins to thicken (but is not too cold!), beat with an electric mixer to soft peaks. If it cools too much before beating, the frosting will harden. Spread on your favorite 6" cake.

There are 1500 calories in Chocolate Ganache Frosting; 250 per ⅙ portion.

Pineapple Upside-Down Cake

Moderate

The light and spongy texture of the cake is the perfect foil for the rich stickiness of the brown sugar and butter that hold the pineapple slices in place. Pineapple Upside-Down Cake is a traditional treat you're sure to enjoy. For a special treat, top with a dollop of whipped cream.

INGREDIENTS

1 recipe Hot Milk Sponge Cake batter (p. 197)

1 tablespoon butter

¼ cup packed brown sugar

1 small can pineapple rings (you'll use 3 of them)

Maraschino cherries and/or pecan halves, optional

DIRECTIONS

1. Preheat the oven to 350°F. Melt the butter in your 6" round cake pan. Stir in the brown sugar and press it down evenly over the bottom of the pan.

2. Arrange the drained pineapple halves in a circle on the brown sugar and butter mixture; chances are three will fit about right. If desired, center a maraschino cherry in the middle of each pineapple ring and/or scatter a few pecan halves over the surface.

3. Prepare the Hot Milk Sponge Cake batter and pour it gently over all. Bake for 25–30 minutes, until the top is puffed, golden, and springs back when lightly touched. Immediately loosen the cake around the edges with a thin spatula and turn out onto your serving plate to cool. If any cherries or pineapple have adhered to the pan, simply lift them off and replace them where they belong.

4. Allow the cake to cool before cutting.

Total calories are 1070 when using 3 cherries; 360 per ⅓ serving or 270 per ¼, before adding cream.

Boston Cream Pie

Moderate–Complex

Boston Cream Pie is a New England classic. The "crust" of the pie is actually fluffy sponge cake, split to encapsulate a custard cream filling. Rich chocolate glaze completes the treat. Be sure to refrigerate your Boston Cream Pie.

INGREDIENTS

1 recipe Hot Milk Sponge Cake (p. 197), baked, cooled, and split horizontally

2 tablespoons cornstarch

¼ cup sugar

Pinch salt

¾ cup half-and-half

1 egg yolk

½ teaspoon vanilla extract

DIRECTIONS

1. Combine the cornstarch, sugar, and salt in a small saucepan, whisking until combined. Whisk in the half-and-half, stirring until smooth.

2. Cook over medium heat, whisking frequently, until the mixture comes to a full boil. Immediately whisk a little of the hot liquid into the egg yolk to temper it. Pour the yolk mixture into the pan and continue to cook, whisking constantly, for a few seconds to cook the yolk and complete the thickening process.

3. Remove from the heat and stir in the vanilla. Once it has cooled slightly, but not completely, spread it on the cut side of the bottom half of the sponge cake, leaving about ½" around the edges. Replace the top half, cut side down. Refrigerate while making the glaze.

The custard filling has 535 calories total.

(continued)

Chocolate Glaze

INGREDIENTS

3 tablespoons half-and-half

1 tablespoon light corn syrup

¼ cup semi-sweet chocolate chips

2 teaspoons unsweetened cocoa powder

¼ cup confectioner's sugar

DIRECTIONS

1. Heat the half-and-half along with the corn syrup to just under boiling. Stir in the chocolate chips until they are completely melted, remove from heat, and then stir in the combined cocoa powder and confectioner's sugar.

2. Pour evenly over the filled Boston Cream Pie, allowing some to dribble down over the edges. This makes a thick, rich chocolate glaze; you may wish to score the top into serving-sized divisions before refrigerating.

The glaze contains 455 calories. Boston Cream Pie total calories: 1660 total 415 per ¼ serving or 275 per ⅙.

A COUPLE OF COOKIES THAT MULTITASK

In the world of small batch baking, cookies face some unique challenges. Fortunately, the following two recipes rise to the occasion. Trifecta Perfecta Cookies begin with a basic dough that is divided into thirds and then embellished with a plethora of combined chocolate chips, nuts, and/or dried fruits. Mix and match any combinations that appeal to you, and freeze what you don't wish to bake right away to enjoy another day. Simple Sugar Cookies produces just six little cookies per batch but includes variations galore, providing you with themed cookies for any number of special occasions.

Trifecta Perfecta Cookies
Moderate

Everyone has his or her favorite variation of a chocolate chip cookie. With this recipe, you're welcome to mix and match chocolate and other delicious additions to your heart's content. A batch of master mix divides easily into three smaller portions, ready to add in any of the below combinations, or invent your own if you prefer. Roll into balls, freeze, seal in plastic bags, and you'll have just the right number to pop into the oven whenever you want a chocolate chip cookie or two. You won't need to worry about leftover stale cookies anymore! Each divided batch produces 6 small cookies or 2 large cookies. So go ahead; enjoy them warm from the oven!

INGREDIENTS

¼ cup soft butter

¼ cup granulated sugar

¼ cup packed brown sugar

2 tablespoons beaten egg (½ egg)

½ teaspoon vanilla extract

⅔ cup all-purpose flour

¼ teaspoon baking soda

¼ teaspoon salt

DIRECTIONS

1. Preheat oven to 375°F. Cream together the butter and sugars until smooth and creamy.

2. Beat in the egg and vanilla until the mixture is light and fluffy.

3. Combine the dry ingredients and stir into the butter and sugar mixture until the dough is smooth and thick.

4. Divide the dough into three equal portions (measure if you wish). Add whatever combination of chocolate chips, nuts, and fruits you wish; suggestions and calorie counts follow. Divide each section of dough into either two larger or six smaller portions, rolling into smooth balls between the palms of your hands.

5. Bake on an ungreased baking sheet. If your oven is full-sized, place the baking sheet on an upper rack. Baking time is 8–10 minutes for small cookies; 15 for large. The cookies will be light brown around the edges but still appear slightly under-baked in the middle, which will make nice chewy cookies. Add a minute or two for frozen dough. The total yield from the entire recipe is 18 small cookies or 6 large.

Total calories before adding chocolate chips, fruits, and nuts: 1170. There are 65 each in 18 small plain cookies and 195 each in 6 large plain cookies. Each ⅓ batch of dough equals 390 calories.

(continued)

TO EACH ⅓ BATCH OF DOUGH ADD:

CHERRY-CHOCOLATE-ALMOND
2 tablespoons each dried snipped cherries,
   semi-sweet chocolate chips, and sliced
   almonds.

> *290 calories + 390 calories = 680 total:115 each in 6 small or 340 each in 2 large cookies.*

APRICOT-MILK CHOCOLATE-PISTACHIO
2 tablespoons each snipped dried apricots,
   milk chocolate chips, and chopped
   pistachios.

> *280 calories + 390 calories = 670 total: 110 each in 6 small or 335 each in 2 large cookies.*

TRIPLE CHOCOLATE
2 tablespoons each semi-sweet, milk, and
   white chocolate chips

> *420 calories + 390 calories = 810 total: 135 each in 6 small or 405 each in 2 large cookies.*

APPROXIMATE CALORIE COUNTS FOR FRUITS, NUTS, AND CHOCOLATE ARE
LISTED BELOW, IF YOU'D LIKE TO EXPERIMENT WITH YOUR OWN COMBINA-
TIONS.

> *Per 2 tablespoons: Dried cranberries 55, Dried cherries 70, chocolate chips 140, almonds 85, pistachios 90, walnuts/pecans 100, snipped dried apricots 50.*

Simple Sugar Cookies
Easy

These simple drop cookies lend themselves to a wide variety of variations, suitable for any occasion from Halloween to Christmas to the Fourth of July. A few of them are suggested below.

INGREDIENTS

2 tablespoons soft butter

2 tablespoons sugar

⅛ teaspoon vanilla extract

2 teaspoons beaten egg

¼ cup flour

⅛ teaspoon baking soda

Dash salt

DIRECTIONS

1. Preheat oven to 375°F. Cream together the butter, sugar, and vanilla until light and fluffy. Add egg and beat until combined.

2. Stir in the combined flour, baking soda, and salt. Chill briefly for easier handling, if you wish.

3. Form into 6 even balls. You may leave the dough balls as they are or roll in plain, colored, or cinnamon sugar. Place on an ungreased cookie sheet and bake at 375°F for 8–10 minutes, until the cookies are puffed and slightly browned around the bottom edges. Loosen with a spatula to cool.

This makes 6 cookies; approximately 315 calories total or 50–55 per plain cookie.

SNICKERDOODLES

1. Roll each ball of dough in cinnamon sugar. Bake as is, or if you wish, make into a Sand Dollar by pressing half a walnut or pecan into the half baked cookies after 5 minutes; continue baking until done.

CHERRY KISS CHRISTMAS COOKIES

1. Roll each ball of dough in green sugar. Bake for 5 minutes; press half a candied red cherry into the center of each and continue baking until done.

(continued)

CANDY CORN COOKIES

1. Bake the plain cookies as directed. Combine 6 tablespoons confectioner's sugar with 2–3 teaspoons orange juice to make a thick glaze. Spoon and smooth evenly over the cooled cookies. Press a piece of candy corn into each cookie.

ROLLED SUGAR COOKIES

1. This dough also rolls out quite nicely. Place the chilled dough on a lightly floured surface, sprinkle a bit of flour over the top and roll out fairly thin; less than ⅛" is about right. Cut out with floured cutters of your choice; the number of cookies will vary depending on the cutter size. If you wish, brush with a little milk and sprinkle with colored sugar. Bake at 375°F for as little as 5 minutes for small, thin cookies; they should be light brown around the edges. Lift carefully with a spatula; place on a mesh rack to cool completely. You can also ice the cookies after they are cool, if you wish.

Calculate calories based on the 315 calorie total divided by the number of cookies you are able to cut from the dough.

BAR COOKIES

While brownies are arguably the best known bar cookie (and there's no arguing that they are delicious!), there are plenty of other tasty bar cookies just waiting to be baked. These cookies lend themselves particularly well to small batch baking; each of the following recipes is geared to be baked in your handy-dandy little 3 cup, 4" x 6" Pyrex pan.

Cocoa Fudge Brownies
Easy

Who doesn't love brownies? This recipe makes just enough of the fudgy little bars for a smaller household. If you wish, feel free to sprinkle a few chocolate chips or chopped nuts over the surface before baking; just be aware the calorie count listed below doesn't include these options.

INGREDIENTS

¼ cup butter

½ cup plus 1 tablespoon sugar

¼ teaspoon vanilla extract

3 tablespoons dark cocoa powder

1 egg

¼ cup flour

1 tablespoon water

DIRECTIONS

1. Preheat oven to 350°F. Melt the butter and stir in the sugar, vanilla, and cocoa. Beat in the egg until well blended.

2. Stir in the flour, and then stir in the water. Pour into a buttered and floured 4" x 6" pan.

3. Bake for about 30 minutes, until the top is glossy and slightly cracked but the brownies are still quite soft to touch. For best results, cool before cutting, although they are quite tasty when served warm topped with a scoop of your favorite ice cream.

This makes 4 generously sized brownies at about 290 calories each, or 1150 total. (If you like nuts or chocolate chips in your brownies, read the calorie count on the packaging; add about ¼ cup to the batter before spreading in the pan.)

Oatmeal Date Bars

Moderate

Traditional date bar cookies are after-school (or work) comfort food. Or, bring them in to share at break time! This variation adds just a bit of orange juice to the date filling for an extra flavor accent.

INGREDIENTS

½ cup chopped dates

¼ cup orange juice

¼ cup water

⅓ cup flour

¼ cup quick cooking rolled oats

2 tablespoons sliced almonds

3 tablespoons packed brown sugar

¼ teaspoon almond extract

¼ cup butter, melted

DIRECTIONS

1. Combine the dates, orange juice, and water in a small saucepan. Bring to a boil and stir frequently, for 2–3 minutes, until the mixture thickens slightly. (It will thicken more on standing.) Set aside to cool for about ½ hour.

2. Preheat oven to 350°F. Combine all the remaining ingredients in a medium mixing bowl, stirring until the mixture becomes crumb-like.

3. Firmly pat about ⅔ of the oat mixture into a well-buttered 4" x 6" pan, making a slight rim around the edges. Carefully pour the date filling over the crust, smoothing almost to the sides. Crumble the remaining oat mixture evenly over all.

4. Bake for approximately 30 minutes, until the crumb crust is lightly browned. Cool slightly before cutting into squares; they will lift from the pan more easily if cooled thoroughly first.

Total calories are about 1120; about 280 calories per ¼ size bar or 140 per ⅛ size bar.

Fruit & Chocolate Oatmeal Bars
Moderate

In this case, jam replaces dates as the filling between layers of sweet, buttery oatmeal crumble. Mini chocolate chips in the filling and a bit of coconut in the crumble make these little bars sweet and memorable.

INGREDIENTS

⅓ cup flour

¼ cup quick cooking rolled oats

3 tablespoons flaked coconut

3 tablespoons packed brown sugar

½ teaspoon vanilla extract

¼ cup butter, melted

¼ cup raspberry, strawberry, or apricot jam

2 tablespoons chocolate mini chips

DIRECTIONS

1. Preheat oven to 350°F. Place everything but the jam and chocolate mini chips in a medium mixing bowl, stirring to combine well; the mixture will be crumbly. Pat about ⅔ of this mixture into a 4" x 6" pan, forming a slight rim around the edges.

2. Carefully spread the jam over the base and sprinkle on the chocolate chips. Crumble the remaining oat mixture evenly over all.

3. Bake for about 30 minutes, until the crust is lightly browned. Cool completely before cutting into squares.

There are about 1200 calories total; 300 calories per ¼ size bar or 200 per ⅙ size bar.

Lemon Squares
Moderate

Light and bright, lemon squares just hit the spot for snacking or dessert. Fresh lemon zest adds an especially nice flavor, if you have a lemon to grate.

INGREDIENTS

¼ cup butter

2 tablespoons confectioner's sugar

½ teaspoon pure lemon extract, divided, or fresh grated lemon zest

½ cup + 1 tablespoon flour, divided

1 large egg

½ cup sugar

3 tablespoons lemon juice

1 tablespoon flour

DIRECTIONS

1. Preheat the oven to 350°F. Cream together the butter, confectioner's sugar, and ¼ teaspoon of the lemon extract or zest.

2. Stir in the ½ cup of flour until well blended and pat firmly into a 6"x 4" baking pan, building a slight rim around the edges. Bake the crust for 10 minutes while preparing the filling.

3. Combine the egg, sugar, lemon juice, 1 tablespoon of flour, and the remaining lemon extract or zest and beat until smooth and light.

4. Pour over the partially baked crust and continue baking for 20–25 minutes longer, until the top is lightly browned and slightly puffed; the filling may look bubbly. Cool completely before cutting into 4 to 8 squares.

There are about 1150 calories total; 290 per ¼ size, 145 per ⅛ size serving.

Rhubarb Squares

Moderate

Here's a nice variation on a rhubarb recipe that may be eaten either as a bar cookie or topped with whipped cream or vanilla ice cream for a more sophisticated dessert. Be sure to dice the walnuts and rhubarb quite fine so that everything cooks evenly and so the squares (or rectangles, to be more accurate) will cut evenly.

INGREDIENTS

¼ cup soft butter

2 tablespoons confectioner's sugar

½ cup + 1 tablespoon flour, divided

2 tablespoons finely diced walnuts

1 large egg

½ cup packed brown sugar

½ cup diced rhubarb

½ teaspoon vanilla extract

⅛ teaspoon cinnamon

DIRECTIONS

1. Preheat oven to 350°F. Cream together the butter and confectioner's sugar until smooth. Stir in the ½ cup flour and walnuts until well blended.

2. Pat evenly into a 6" x 4" baking pan, forming a slightly elevated rim around all the edges. Bake for 5–10 minutes, while preparing the filling.

3. Combine the egg, brown sugar, 1 tablespoon flour, vanilla, and cinnamon, beating with an electric mixer until light and fluffy.

4. Fold in the rhubarb and pour into the partially baked filling. Bake another 25–30 minutes, until the filling is evenly golden and slightly puffed. Remove from the oven and cool before cutting.

This makes 4 good-sized squares or 8 cookie-sized squares at about 1000 calories per pan; 250 calories per ¼ square or 125 calories per ⅛ square (not counting ice cream or whipped cream).

Peanut Butterscotch Bars

Easy

These cookie bars are a snap to make and addictively delicious. If they have any drawback, it might be the calories involved in consuming them; these are definitely not diet fare! However, for an occasional indulgence, they're hard to beat.

INGREDIENTS

2 tablespoons butter, divided

3 double graham crackers, crushed to ½ cup crumbs

½ cup butterscotch morsels

¼ cup shredded coconut

3 tablespoons crunchy peanut butter

½ cup sweetened condensed milk

DIRECTIONS

1. Place the pan and 1 tablespoon of the butter in the oven while it's preheating to 350°F. Once it has melted, remove and sprinkle the graham cracker crumbs evenly over the entire surface.

2. Sprinkle the butterscotch morsels over the graham cracker crumbs, followed by the flaked coconut.

3. In a small saucepan over low heat, melt together the remaining 1 tablespoon of butter and the peanut butter until they become liquid. Pour this mixture evenly over the contents of the pan. Finally, pour the condensed milk evenly over all.

4. Bake for 20–25 minutes, until the top is golden brown and bubbly. Cool thoroughly before cutting.

There are about 1785 calories total, or about 225 per ⅛ size serving.

FESTIVE FEASTS

Let's celebrate! Special occasions are part of what makes life pleasurable, and much of what makes them special revolves around food. Here is a collection of special occasion menus and recipes made small enough so that you needn't worry about eating leftovers indefinitely after each event. With a few exceptions for some of the more traditional meals, where you expect to spend a little extra time in the kitchen, they've also been streamlined to allow you plenty of time to relax and enjoy the day . . . or night!

NEW YEAR'S EVE STEAK DINNER

Chances are you don't want to be spending hours in the kitchen on New Year's Eve, and with this festive dinner you needn't. The potato can be prepared a day or two in advance, wrapped in foil, and stored in the fridge; allow a few extra minutes' baking time to ensure they're heated through. The bread may also be spread with the onion mixture in advance and stored, wrapped, at room temperature until you're ready to top it with cheese and broil. The cheesecake is actually better made a day or two in advance, which leaves you with only the lettuce wedge and the steak to prepare. Simply use the time while the potato is baking to cook the steak and you're good to go. Happy New Year!

(Lettuce Wedge with favorite dressing)
Cheesy Onion Bread
Steak and Mushrooms
Twice-Baked Cheddar Potato
Tuxedo Cheesecake
(Beverages of choice)

Cheesy Onion Bread
Easy

This savory bread also makes a great accompaniment to spaghetti and other Italian style dishes; or you could serve it with a bowl of steaming soup. Split one loaf between the two of you, or double the recipe if you'd each like your own.

INGREDIENTS

2 teaspoons butter

2 teaspoons olive oil

½ teaspoon instant minced onion

2 teaspoons water

3–4 shakes Tabasco or other pepper sauce

6–8" baguette or submarine style loaf, split lengthwise

1 tablespoon finely grated Parmesan cheese

DIRECTIONS

1. Melt the butter in a small saucepan. Stir in the olive oil, onion, water, and Tabasco. Spread evenly over the cut sides of the bread.

2. Sprinkle with the grated cheese. Broil for 2–3 minutes, until lightly browned.

There are about 400 calories per baguette, or share one for 200 calories each.

Twice-Baked Cheddar Potatoes

Moderate

If you're not a big meat eater, you could serve these as your main course, accompanied by the glazed mushrooms, sans steak. Either way, they're rich and satisfying.

INGREDIENTS

2 (5-ounce) russet baking potatoes, scrubbed

2 teaspoons butter

1 tablespoon sour cream

2 tablespoons shredded sharp cheddar cheese

2 teaspoons minced chives

Sea salt and black pepper

Paprika for topping

DIRECTIONS

1. Pre-cook the potatoes in a microwave for 7–8 minutes, until they are barely tender. Allow the potatoes to rest in the microwave for about ½ hour to finish the cooking process and cool to around room temperature.

2. Place the potatoes flat on a small baking sheet or pan and cut a narrow slice of skin from the top side of each. Carefully scoop out the cooked potato, leaving a thin lining of potato within.

3. Mash the potato with the butter until smooth and creamy. Stir in the sour cream, cheddar cheese, chives, and salt and pepper to taste.

4. Pile the mashed filling back into the skin, smoothing the top and criss-crossing it by lightly running the tines of a fork over the surface.

5. Sprinkle with paprika and bake in a 400°F oven for about 20 minutes, until nicely heated through.

Each potato has about 210 calories.

Steak and Mushrooms

Moderate

Steak is a great choice for festive occasions; adding mushrooms and a flavorful glaze completes this special culinary offering.

INGREDIENTS

Two 4–6-ounce filet mignon or strip steaks,
  1" thick
Cracked black pepper and sea salt
2 tablespoons butter, divided
4 ounces baby portabella mushrooms
1 teaspoon olive oil

2 teaspoons lemon juice
2 teaspoons Worcestershire sauce
¼ cup deglazing liquid: broth, red wine,
  vegetable cooking water
Fresh lemon wedges, optional

DIRECTIONS

1. Use two separate medium skillets or frying pans; cast iron is best. Wipe the mushrooms clean with a damp paper towel. Season the steak to preference with salt and pepper.

2. Place 1 tablespoon butter in one pan; heat over medium high until it is foamy. Add the mushrooms and sauté, stirring occasionally, for 5 minutes, until the mushrooms take on a shiny appearance.

3. Meanwhile heat 1 tablespoon butter and 1 teaspoon olive oil in the second pan over medium high heat. Place the seasoned steak in the pan and cook for approximately 3 minutes, until the first side is nicely browned. Flip the steak over, turn the heat down to medium, and cook until it is done to your liking, about 2–3 minutes longer for medium rare.

4. While the steak finishes cooking, add the lemon juice, a sprinkle of salt, and the Worcestershire sauce to the mushrooms; continue sautéing them for 2–3 minutes longer, until they have formed a glaze. Plate the steak and deglaze the pan with the desired liquid. Pour this over the mushrooms and cook just a minute longer, to form a sauce.

5. Pour the mushrooms and sauce over the steak. Garnish with fresh lemon wedges, if desired, and enjoy.

There are about 500 calories per serving when using a 5-ounce strip steak.

Tuxedo Cheesecake

Moderate

If you don't own a small spring-form pan, it is also possible to bake your cheesecake in a 6" round cake pan. Be sure to line the pan completely with foil that overhangs the edges, and butter the foil very well. Once the cheesecake has baked and chilled, but before the glaze is applied, gently turn the cheesecake out upside down, peel the foil away, and then invert it onto your serving plate. It's possible to do this because this particular cheesecake has such a small diameter; a large one would most likely break apart in your hands.

Fiori di Sicilia is a vanilla and citrus flavoring available from King Arthur Flour. It's fairly intense but imparts a lovely flavor when used with discretion. You can also simply substitute vanilla extract and a bit of orange or lemon zest or flavoring.

INGREDIENTS

4 crisp chocolate cream-filled sandwich cookies

1 tablespoon butter, melted

8 ounces cream cheese, softened

¼ cup sugar

⅛ teaspoon Fiori di Sicilia or ½ teaspoon vanilla extract and ¼ teaspoon shredded orange or lemon zest

1 large egg

4 tablespoons heavy cream, divided

2 ounces semi-sweet bar chocolate (not chips)

Strawberries, raspberries, or cherries for garnish, optional

DIRECTIONS

1. Preheat oven to 325°F. Seal the cookies in a plastic sandwich bag and crush them with a rolling pin or the palm of your hand until they are fine crumbs. Pour the crumbs over the melted butter and mix well. Press lightly into the bottom of a 6" buttered spring form pan.

2. Beat the cream cheese in a small mixing bowl until smooth. Add the sugar and flavorings and beat again. Add the egg and 2 tablespoons heavy cream and beat until smooth and fluffy.

(continued)

3.   Pour over the pressed cookie crust; it will fill right up to the top of the pan. Bake for 35–40 minutes until the top is puffed out, the surface light golden, and the cheesecake is firm but still wiggly. Allow to cool thoroughly before adding the tuxedo glaze.

4.   Heat the remaining 2 tablespoons of heavy cream just to boiling. Remove from the heat and stir in the chopped chocolate until it's all melted. Pour evenly over the chilled cheesecake, smoothing with a spatula. Just before serving, garnish with fresh fruit or berries of your choice.

There are about 1850 total calories in Tuxedo Cheesecake; 465 per ¼ serving; 310 per ⅙ serving without fruit.

VALENTINE'S DAY DELIGHT

Here's a Valentine's themed dinner with hearts and strawberries abounding. Again, many components of it can be prepared in advance, such as the artichokes, aioli, and the sorbet for the cocktails. The salad and dressing may also be prepared in advance; just don't pour the dressing on until the last minute. Even the mini cakes can be prepared a day ahead; the recipe includes tips for reheating them. So, while the artichoke grills and the shrimps broil, fluff the rice and take time to smell the roses. . . .

True Love Champagne Cocktails
Strawberry Spinach Salad (p. 85)
Baked Stuffed Shrimp
Herbed Rice (p. 167)
Grilled Artichoke with Lemon Basil Aioli
Molten Chocolate Mini Cakes

True Love Champagne Cocktails
Easy

The strawberry sorbet requires no ice cream maker; simply stir it periodically while it's freezing. This makes enough sorbet balls for several servings of champagne. They also make a nice component of fruit salad or may simply be enjoyed on their own.

INGREDIENTS

Chilled champagne of choice

Fresh strawberries

Strawberry Sorbet Balls (recipe follows)

DIRECTIONS

1. Place two or three sorbet balls in each champagne flute.

2. Gently pour chilled champagne over the sorbet; garnish with a fresh strawberry or two and serve.

(continued)

Strawberry Sorbet Balls

INGREDIENTS

1 cup washed hulled strawberries, diced

1 tablespoon sugar

1 tablespoon orange juice

1 teaspoon orange liqueur, optional

DIRECTIONS

1. Combine all ingredients in a small bowl or glass measuring cup. Whirl smooth with an immersion blender. Pour into a small container, such as a 3 cup Pyrex pan. Freeze until partially solidified, about 1–1 ½ hours.

2. Stir to blend the frozen and liquid purée together. Freeze and repeat this step 3–4 more times; the length in between will be considerably shorter as the mixture freezes harder.

3. Once the mixture is mostly frozen but still soft enough to scoop, form it into small mounds on a wax paper–lined cake or pie tin; a melon baller or similar implement works well for this.

4. Freeze solid; remove from wax paper and store in the freezer in a sealable plastic bag.

There are about 110 calories in the entire batch of sorbet.

Baked Stuffed Shrimp

Moderate

Here's a classic main course treat for two. You can easily get the prep work done on the shrimp earlier in the day and store it, covered, in the fridge. You may either prepare the cracker stuffing in advance as well and store it in a separate container, or put it together just before broiling the shrimp; it won't take very long to prepare.

INGREDIENTS

4 jumbo (4–6 count) shrimp

2 tablespoons plus 2 teaspoons butter, divided

¼ teaspoon finely minced garlic or
  ⅛ teaspoon garlic powder

1 teaspoon lemon juice

½ teaspoon parsley flakes

½ teaspoon Worcestershire sauce

8 buttery round crackers, crushed

Paprika

Fresh lemon wedges, optional

DIRECTIONS

1. Preheat oven to 400°F. Peel the raw shrimp, leaving the tail intact. Butterfly the shrimp by cutting the shrimp horizontally along its midsection, not quite all the way through. There will be two small string-like membranes you can pull out; a white one when you begin cutting and another, darker one when you're just about through. Place the butterflied shrimp cut side up on an oiled or sprayed baking sheet.

2. In a small saucepan, melt the 2 tablespoons of butter along with the minced garlic. Remove from heat and stir in the lemon juice, parsley, and Worcestershire sauce. Stir in the crushed cracker crumbs, combining thoroughly.

3. Heap the mixture evenly on each of the shrimp and sprinkle lightly with paprika. Bake for 10 minutes.

4. Divide the remaining 2 teaspoons of butter evenly, adding a small pat of it to the top of each shrimp. Continue to bake for 5 more minutes, until the filling is lightly browned and the shrimp has curled slightly and turned pink and white. Serve hot with lemon wedges, if you wish.

There are about 570 calories total in this dish or 285 in each serving.

Grilled Artichoke with Lemon Basil Aioli
Moderate

Special celebrations deserve special veggies as well! Big, beautiful artichokes blend perfectly with zesty aioli in this festive offering. An added benefit of this dish is that almost all steps may be done in advance, leaving only a brief grilling or browning step just before serving.

INGREDIENTS

1 large artichoke

1 tablespoon + 1½ teaspoons lemon juice, divided

¼ teaspoon sea salt

¼ teaspoon shredded lemon zest

¼ teaspoon finely minced garlic

1 very fresh large egg yolk (use pasteurized if you're concerned about salmonella)

¼ teaspoon Dijon mustard

3 tablespoons olive oil

2 tablespoons minced fresh basil leaves

Extra olive oil, salt, and fresh ground black pepper

DIRECTIONS

Either the day before or a few hours in advance, cut the artichoke in half, remove the fuzzy "choke" center, and trim sharp/tough leaf ends. Place in a saucepan just to fit with water to cover and 1 tablespoon of the lemon juice. Make sure there's about 1–2" of clearance at the top so it won't boil over.

1. Cover the pan and bring to a boil over high heat. Reduce the heat to medium low and slow boil for about 20–25 minutes, until the artichoke halves are just tender. Remove from heat, drain, and cool to room temperature. Wrap in plastic or place in a covered container and refrigerate until ready to use.

2. Prepare the aioli: Mash together the salt, lemon zest, and garlic in a small mixing bowl. Stir in the egg yolk, 1½ teaspoons lemon juice, and the Dijon mustard.

3. Now comes the only slightly tricky part. Using a wire whisk, very gradually drizzle in the olive oil, one tablespoon at a time, whisking constantly. You need to add the oil very slowly in order for the sauce to become smooth and creamy; adding it too quickly may result in a separated aioli. Once all the oil has been added, stir in the minced basil.

(continued)

4. Serve at once or cover and refrigerate for a few hours if you prefer to prepare in advance. When ready to enjoy, sprinkle the artichoke halves with olive oil, salt, and pepper. Grill cut side down or broil cut side up for about 3–4 minutes, until they're heated through and lightly browned. You can even brown them in a heavy frying pan over high heat on the stovetop if you prefer.

5. Serve your halves with a dollop of lemon basil aioli in the center of each. If you wish to eat one at a time, broil or grill half, leaving the other in the fridge, and use half the sauce. Plan to use the rest within 2 days.

The aioli contains 405 calories and the artichoke 65 calories for about 470 calories in all or 235 in each serving.

Molten Chocolate Mini Cakes
Moderate

Something as decadent and delicious as Molten Chocolate Mini Cakes is perhaps wiser to prepare in small batches. That makes us a little less prone to temptation. However, for a splurge, or to share with a special someone, they're so worth it. Wrap leftovers, plate and all, with plastic wrap. To enjoy your mini cake another day, simply remove the plastic wrap, make sure it's on a microwavable plate, and microwave on high for about 30 seconds.

INGREDIENTS

3 tablespoons butter

2 ounces bittersweet chocolate, coarsely chopped

¼ teaspoon vanilla extract

½ cup confectioner's sugar

2 tablespoons plus 2 teaspoons all-purpose flour

1 egg plus 1 egg yolk

Vanilla ice cream

Strawberry Blackberry Sauce

DIRECTIONS

1. Butter or spray generously with non-stick cooking spray 2 6-ounce custard cups; place on a baking sheet and set aside.

2. Preheat your oven to 425°F. Melt together the butter and bittersweet chocolate, either by microwaving for one minute or heating gently over indirect heat. Stir until the chocolate is fully melted and the mixture is smooth.

3. Stir in the vanilla and then stir in the confectioner's sugar and the flour. Last, beat in the egg and the egg yolk. The mixture should be shiny and smooth.

4. Divide evenly between the two buttered custard cups. Place the baking sheet with the filled cups into the preheated oven and bake for approximately 12 minutes, until the top is shiny, the edges firm, and the center is slightly cracked but also liquid is appearing.

5. Remove from the oven, carefully slide a flat spatula or knife blade around each mini cake, and turn out onto two serving plates. If you wish, each mini molten cake can be cut in half and placed on separate plates. Serve warm with vanilla ice cream and a spoonful of Strawberry Blackberry Sauce. This recipe serves 2–4, depending . . .

One mini cake by itself is 540 calories; divided between two, it is 270 apiece.

(continued)

Strawberry Blackberry Sauce

INGREDIENTS

½ cup fresh or frozen loose pack strawberries

½ cup fresh or frozen loose pack blackberries

1 tablespoon sugar

1 tablespoon orange flavored liqueur or
orange juice

DIRECTIONS

1. Slice the strawberries and, if very large, cut the blackberries in half. Stir them together in a small bowl with the sugar and liqueur or juice.

2. Allow the mixture to macerate while you're preparing your molten mini cakes; then spoon them on and enjoy!

Because berries are relatively low calorie on the dessert scale, this entire batch of sauce comes in at under 200 calories even when using liqueur; if using orange juice, it's only about 150.

EASTER SUNDAY DINNER

As with so many special occasions, you're going to want time to enjoy the day, even if you love to cook. With a little planning, you'll have that time. You'll want to hard cook a few extra eggs in advance, so the jellied salad can be prepared the day before. The potatoes can also be constructed up to a day in advance, covered, and refrigerated, and popped in the oven to bake along with the ham. Pastel de Tres Leches is definitely a day-ahead kind of cake; just save the garnishes for the last minute. The rolls can be baked a day in advance and re-heated, or you could leave the dough to rise while you're at church or hunting Easter eggs, then form and bake them along with or just after the potatoes and ham.

Lemon Jellied Easter Eggs
Baked Easter Mini Ham
Individual Pommes Anna
(Steamed or Grilled Asparagus)
Crescent Rolls (p. 57)
Pastel de Tres Leches

Lemon Jellied Easter Eggs

Complex

This pretty yellow jellied salad tastes as bright and refreshing as it looks. Depending on how egg-enriched you'd like it, you may either use just two eggs, suspended in the clear lemon jell, or add an additional egg, chopped up, to the cottage cheese and mayonnaise jelled layer. (Powdered sumac may be hard to find. Although it will enhance the citrusy flavor of the salad, don't worry if you don't have access; it is also quite tasty without it.)

INGREDIENTS

1 package unflavored gelatin

6 tablespoons sugar

⅛ teaspoon salt

⅛ teaspoon paprika

⅛ teaspoon powdered sumac, optional

1½ cups water, divided

¼ cup fresh or frozen thawed lemon juice

2–3 hard cooked eggs

1 tablespoon finely diced green pepper, optional

1 tablespoon finely diced celery

1 teaspoon snipped chives

¼ cup cottage cheese

A few grinds of black pepper

1 tablespoon mayonnaise

Bits of celery leaves, chives, and/or green pepper bits for decoration

DIRECTIONS

1. Soften the gelatin in ¼ cup of cold water for 2–3 minutes. Combine the sugar, salt, paprika, powdered sumac if using, and ½ cup water in a small saucepan; bring to a boil.

2. Stir in the softened gelatin, continuing to stir until it has thoroughly dissolved. Remove from the heat and add the lemon juice and ¾ cup of cold water. Chill the mixture until it starts to set but is still a thick liquid.

3. Spray a small gelatin mold or Pyrex casserole dish (2–2½ cups) with non-stick spray, or lightly oil it. Carefully pour ¼ cup of the gelatin mixture into the mold; refrigerate.

4. Shell the eggs and halve two of them lengthwise. Place the halves, cut side down, on the gelatin base, forming a design of your choice and pressing down slightly. Carefully pour another ¼ cup of semi-liquid gelatin over the eggs and chill.

5. When mostly set, press vegetable garnishes of choice into the soft set gelatin. Add another ¼ cup of semi-liquid gelatin and again chill until mostly set. Meanwhile, chop the third egg, if you choose to use it, and combine with the green pepper, celery, chives, cottage cheese, and a grind or two of pepper.

6. Whisk the mayonnaise into the remaining gelatin mixture until it is well integrated; by this time the gelatin should be semi-set. Fold the cottage cheese mixture into the gelatin and pour over the egg halves set in the gelatin base. Chill at least two hours; overnight is even better. Dip in hot water briefly to unmold. Cut in quarters to serve, or smaller pieces if you're enjoying a large meal.

There are about 550 calories in the entire salad or about 140 in each quarter serving.

Baked Easter Mini Ham

Easy-Moderate

Fortunately for smaller households, there are now petite cuts referred to as "quarter hams" available. These are fully cooked and often even pre-sliced, and are great for glazing in the oven. One mini ham will feed the two of you generously with a goodly amount of leftovers for sandwiches and such. Due to the ham's smaller size, a slightly higher oven temperature helps to ensure that the ham glaze will caramelize nicely during the heating process.

INGREDIENTS

1½–2-pound quarter ham

Small (4 slice) can of pineapple

2 tablespoons pineapple juice, drained from the can

¼ cup packed brown sugar

Pinch each of ginger and cloves

1 teaspoon prepared mustard

4 maraschino cherries, optional

DIRECTIONS

1. Preheat oven to 375°F. Place the ham in a small baking dish. Arrange the pineapple slices evenly over the ham and place a cherry in the center of each slice, attaching with wooden toothpicks if need be. Combine the rest of the ingredients and pour about half evenly over the ham.

2. Add water to the bottom of the pan—just enough to prevent the glaze from burning once it drips to the bottom. Bake for approximately 60 minutes total, basting once or twice with the remaining glaze. The ham should be heated through and the glaze slightly caramelized in appearance.

3. Remove to a serving platter and allow it to rest for 5–10 minutes. Heat the pan drippings (with a small amount of water or vegetable cooking liquid if need be); transfer to a small gravy boat or dish and serve with the ham.

Each 4-ounce serving of ham without glaze is about 140 calories; the total calorie count for the fruit and glaze is about 320–350 calories.

Individual Pommes Anna

Moderate

Try using mini pie plates for cooking this butter rich potato dish; each one is just right for a single serving. Although the slightly higher oven temperature is optimal for baking Pommes Anna, they will cook quite nicely along with the ham at 375°F.

INGREDIENTS

2 tablespoons butter

2 russet potatoes, about 5 ounces each

Freshly ground salt and pepper

Crumbled rosemary

DIRECTIONS

1. Preheat oven to 375–400°F. Melt the butter in a small pan; use just a little to butter the bottom and side of a 4" pie plate. Peel the potato and slice as thinly and uniformly as possible. A mandoline is desirable for this, although the wide bar on a grater may also be used. Be cautious and use a buffer between your hand and the slicing device. If need be, you can also slice the potato with a sharp knife, again as thinly as possible without cutting a finger in the process.

2. Place the sliced potatoes in a layer of concentric rings in the bottom of the pie plate. Sprinkle with salt, pepper, and a small pinch of rosemary. Drizzle a little butter over the top. Repeat twice more to make 3 layers, seasoning and drizzling the potatoes with butter each time.

3. Place a small square of buttered foil over the top of the pie plate, crimping around the edges, and bake for 30 minutes. Remove the foil, pushing the potatoes down into the pan. Continue baking for 30 minutes longer, until the potatoes are golden and tender.

4. To serve, loosen the potatoes gently with a knife or spatula and turn out of the pan upside down to enjoy.

There are about 240 calories per serving.

Pastel de Tres Leches

Moderate-Complex

This cake is very popular in Latin America, where the recipe originated. It utilizes three kinds of "milk" . . . in this instance, evaporated and condensed milks and heavy cream, which are allowed to soak into the surface of the baked cake, moistening and enriching it. When ready to serve, it's topped with a fluffy citrus scented meringue and fresh seasonal fruits and berries. This recipe will make enough to have seconds. It's a great "festive" dessert for a special event.

INGREDIENTS

1 recipe Hot Milk Sponge Cake, baked and cooled (p. 197)

¼ cup evaporated milk

¼ cup sweetened condensed milk

¼ cup heavy cream

1 tablespoon light rum or 1 teaspoon vanilla extract

½ cup sugar

1 tablespoon light corn syrup

3 tablespoons water

Pinch salt

1 egg white

2 teaspoons lime juice

¼ teaspoon grated lime zest

Fresh berries and fruits: strawberries, blueberries, blackberries, peaches, mangoes, etc.

DIRECTIONS

1. Loosen the cooled cake around the edges; remove from the pan, placing the parchment circle back in the bottom of the pan for the next step. Replace the cake in the pan and pierce the top all over with a sharp thin knife or skewer.

2. Combine the evaporated milk, condensed milk, heavy cream, and rum or vanilla in a small bowl. Slowly and evenly pour it over the cake, allowing it to soak in. Cover the cake pan with plastic wrap or foil and refrigerate for at least 8 hours, or up to 2 days.

3. At least ½ hour before serving, combine the sugar, corn syrup, water, and salt in a small saucepan. Bring to a boil, using the small burner if your stove has one, stirring occasionally. Once it has come to a full boil, allow it to boil over medium heat without stirring for 3 full minutes; swirl the pan occasionally if you feel the heating process is becoming uneven.

4. Meanwhile, combine the egg white and lime juice in a small heatproof mixing bowl and beat until the mixture is foamy. Pour the boiling hot sugar mixture over the egg white, beating constantly, and continue to beat for about 2 minutes, until the frosting is fluffy white and thick. Stir in the lime zest.

5. Invert the cake onto a serving plate and cover generously with the fluffy lime frosting. Top with the fresh fruits of your choice and either serve immediately or refrigerate until serving time. Although it will keep a few days in the refrigerator, Pastel de Tres Leches is best when it is served fresh.

The cake and meringue topping without fruit equals about 1700 calories or 425 per ¼ size serving;
285 per ⅙ size serving.

FOURTH OF JULY FUN

Who doesn't love Independence Day? And who doesn't love a cookout? Add them together and you have a winning combination! This menu is perfect for a backyard cookout, and with a few accommodations it can be transported to your favorite beach or picnic area.

Fruit Kebabs with Citrus Cream
Burgers Deluxe
(Corn on the Cob)
(Assorted Chips)
S'mores Sundaes

Fruit Kebabs with Citrus Cream

Moderate

Wooden skewers work well for constructing your kebabs, although toothpicks can be used for mini kebabs. If it's easier, simply serve the fruit alongside the dip with a fork for each person. This makes a generous amount of dip, enough for more than one meal, or see the suggestions at the end of the recipe for other uses.

INGREDIENTS

1 lemon

1 orange

1 lime or grapefruit

½ cup sugar

1 egg

¼ cup butter

½ or ¼ cup sour cream

Assorted fruits for dipping

DIRECTIONS

1. For this recipe, you will need ¼ cup of combined lemon, orange, and lime or grapefruit juice and 2 teaspoons of mixed citrus zest. Err on the side of more lemon if you're conflicted about proportions, and remember to save unused orange and grapefruit sections for the fruit skewers. Combine the juice, sugar, and egg in a small saucepan, whisking well. Bring to a boil over medium heat, continuing to whisk constantly so the mixture doesn't burn, and cook until it has slightly thickened.

2. Remove from the heat and whisk in the butter and citrus zest. Cool completely; this can be accomplished more rapidly by placing the small pan into a larger flat container partially filled with cold water. Cover and refrigerate until just before serving time.

3. This will make just about a cup of dip base, which when mixed with the ½ cup of sour cream may provide a more generous quantity than you wish to use all at once. If this is the case, you can divide it in half, stirring in ¼ cup of sour cream, and save the rest to mix and enjoy another day. Because the base is essentially a fruit curd, you could also opt to leave the other half as is and enjoy it spread over hot biscuits, English muffins, or vanilla cake. To serve, cut fruits of your choice into bite-sized pieces and skewer, along with strawberries and/or grapes, for dipping.

There are about 800 calories in the base; 1000 per 1½ cups of dip or 125 per ¼ cup serving.

Burger Deluxe
Easy-Moderate

This is one recipe where the pre-made beef patties come in handy; each will provide you with a generously sized burger. Between the burger, bun, and cheese each will also average about 500 calories; the lettuce and tomato add very few to this amount. If you prefer a non-beef burger, feel free to substitute whatever ground meat or meatless substitute you wish. Calorie counts for each of the spreads are listed after the individual recipes.

INGREDIENTS

2 (5–6 ounce) Black Angus or other high-quality ground beef patties (85% lean)

Coarse ground salt and pepper

2–4 slices Muenster cheese

2 toasted kaiser buns

Thinly sliced tomato

Leaf lettuce

Avocado Spread

Burger Deluxe Spread

Pickles and/or olives, optional

DIRECTIONS

1. Prepare the spreads up to a day in advance, if you wish; cover tightly and refrigerate.

2. Grill the burger to your liking, sprinkling generously with salt and pepper; toast the bun at the same time. Place the cheese on top of the burger about a minute before it's done, so that the cheese melts but doesn't run all over the place.

3. To assemble, spread a dollop of Burger Deluxe Spread on the bottom of the bun and top with the leaf lettuce. Place the burger on top, followed by the tomato, the Avocado Spread, and the top bun. Serve at once, garnished with olives and/or pickles, if desired.

(continued)

Avocado Spread

INGREDIENTS

½ Hass avocado

¼ teaspoon cumin

⅛ teaspoon salt

1 teaspoon lime or lemon juice

DIRECTIONS

1. Mash together the peeled and pitted avocado, cumin, salt, and lime or lemon juice until it's a smooth as you'd like.

2. Spread on burgers.

This makes about 3–4 tablespoons of spread; about 240 calories, or 120 per serving.

Burger Deluxe Spread

INGREDIENTS

2 tablespoons mayonnaise

2 tablespoons ketchup

1 teaspoon coarse Dijon or brown mustard

½ teaspoon Worcestershire sauce

½ teaspoon instant minced onion

DIRECTIONS

1. Combine all ingredients in a small bowl. Cover and refrigerate until serving time; this improves if made at least ½ hour in advance.

2. Spread on burgers.

There are about 240 calories per batch in this recipe, or 120 per serving.

S'mores Sundaes

Easy

This recipe is easiest to make where you have access to a small broiler, as the mini marshmallows are a bit tricky to toast over an open fire. If you wish to be adventurous and toast whole marshmallows instead, I'd still suggest using a dab of marshmallow spread to anchor each to the graham cracker before constructing the sundaes. And, if you don't have marshmallow spread, feel free to substitute a dab of peanut butter or chocolate hazelnut spread in its place; either will add a nice layer of flavor to this yummy ice cream treat. If you've headed off to a picnic area, better plan to pack the ice cream very well in ice . . . or possibly just save the sundaes for an at-home treat later in the day.

INGREDIENTS

1 cup chocolate ice cream

4 graham cracker squares

2 tablespoons marshmallow spread

4 tablespoons mini marshmallows

6 tablespoons Warm Milk Chocolate Sauce

Whipped cream

DIRECTIONS

1. Spread the graham crackers evenly with the marshmallow spread and press the mini marshmallows evenly over the top. Place under the broiler for a minute or two, until they are lightly browned and puffed.

2. Meanwhile, scoop the ice into two serving bowls. Once the marshmallow grahams are ready, place them on top of the ice cream. Drizzle with the warm chocolate sauce and top with a dollop or squirt of whipped cream.

Each sundae is about 560 calories before adding cream; a ¼ cup dollop of sweetened whipped cream will add about 125 more; if you use spray whipped cream instead check the container for calorie count.

(continued)

Warm Milk Chocolate Sauce

⅓ cup half-and-half

1 cup milk chocolate chips or morsels

1. Heat the half-and-half just to boiling. Remove from heat and stir in the milk chocolate chips until they melt and the sauce is smooth.

2. Serve at once or cover and refrigerate for later; reheat in the microwave 20 seconds at a time until it is warmed through (for best results, do not boil). If you're picnicking away from home, pour the warm sauce into a thermos or bring along a small saucepan and warm it up on the edge of the fire.

This makes ¾ cup of sauce; approximately 1200 calories or 100 calories per tablespoon.

BIRTHDAY BRUNCH

Although this brunch seems somewhat slanted toward summer, it's a great way to celebrate any time of the year. The latte recipe even includes variations for a hot or chilled treat. Prepare the soup and cake a day in advance, and chill your coffee, if you're planning on iced lattes. Start the potatoes after preparing the béchamel sauce and just before constructing the Croques and everything should come out just about right.

The day before brunch, prepare your favorite cake and frosting from the Delectable Desserts section. If you wish, decorate with edible, non-sprayed flowers, fresh fruits or berries, and/or assorted little candies. Jelly beans, pastel mints, plain or pastel colored mini marshmallows, candy-coated bite-sized chocolate candies, or chocolate encased truffles, cut in half, are all good possibilities. Or, if you're handy with a cake decorating kit, by all means decorate away!

Chilled Cantaloupe Soup

Croques Madame or Monsieur

Potatoes O'Brien

Snowy White Cake or Dark Chocolate Cake (p. 198 and 201)

Hazelnut Mocha Latte

Chilled Cantaloupe Soup
Easy

This cool, pastel orange soup is a great way to begin, or end, a summer day. It's a snap to make, as long as you have a blender of some sort to make it nice and smooth. Although cardamom may not be a spice you keep on hand, I really do recommend picking a bit up for this recipe; in many natural foods stores it's possible to buy just a small quantity at a time. Cardamom also adds a nice flavor to homemade cinnamon buns or cinnamon toast, or try sprinkling a little bit into a cup of hot tea with milk.

INGREDIENTS

2 cups cantaloupe chunks

¼ cup plain Greek yogurt

2 tablespoons lime juice

2 tablespoons honey

¼ teaspoon ground cardamom

½ cup orange juice

Fresh mint leaves, chiffonaded or left whole, for garnish (optional)

DIRECTIONS

1. Combine all ingredients in a blender, or use an immersion blender in a small bowl. Blend until smooth.

2. The soup may be served immediately or chilled, covered, up to overnight. Garnish with fresh mint leaves for extra color and flavor.

This refreshing soup is about 170 calories per serving.

Croque Monsieur or Madame

Moderate

Croque Monsieur, colloquially known as Crispy Mister, is a variation on grilled ham and cheese traditionally utilizing Gruyère cheese. In many versions, including this one, a creamy béchamel sauce covers the grilled sandwich, adding a luxuriant extra layer of flavor and texture. Croque Madame, Monsieur's female counterpart, tops everything off with a lightly fried egg. Because this is such a rich recipe, I prefer to use a lighter version of bread in it, although any firm white bread may be used. The light Italian bread counts for about 80 calories in this recipe, so if you choose to substitute a different variety, simply adjust the count accordingly. You needn't wait until your birthday to enjoy this slightly decadent sandwich, although it's sure to make your special day even more special.

INGREDIENTS

2 tablespoon plus 2 teaspoon butter, divided

4 teaspoons flour

⅔ cup milk

¼ teaspoon salt

Fresh ground pepper

Pinch nutmeg

4 slices light Italian style sandwich bread

Dijon mustard (preferably coarse grain)

4 ounces thinly sliced ham or smoked turkey

5 ounces (1¼ cup) shredded Gruyère cheese

Paprika and/or chopped chives

Optional for Madame, 2 eggs plus 2 teaspoon butter

DIRECTIONS

1. Prepare the béchamel: Melt 2 teaspoons of butter in a small saucepan over medium heat. Stir in the flour and cook for a minute or two. Whisk in the milk all at once, along with the salt and a small pinch each of pepper and nutmeg. Cook over medium heat, whisking constantly, until the sauce thickens and bubbles; set aside to stay warm.

2. Spread two slices of bread with 1 teaspoon of the butter on each; place butter side down in a heavy frying pan. Spread the top lightly with mustard; top with the sliced ham.

3. Sprinkle 1 cup of the cheese evenly on top of the ham and top with the other slices of bread. If you wish, smear just a bit of the béchamel on the inside of the second slice of bread before topping the grated cheese with it.

(continued)

4. Grill over medium heat until the bottom sides are golden brown. While they're grilling on one side, spread the top sides with another teaspoon of butter; carefully turn and grill until browned on the second sides as well.

5. Place the hot grilled sandwiches on heatproof plates or a baking sheet. Pour the béchamel evenly over the tops and sprinkle with the remaining Gruyère. Broil for a minute or two, until the cheese just bubbles. If you wish to have a Croque Madame, fry the eggs gently in two teaspoons of butter until they're done to your liking, seasoning to taste with salt and pepper, while the sandwiches are broiling.

6. Remove to serving plates, sprinkle with paprika and/or chives, top with the eggs, if desired, and serve immediately.

Croque Monsieur has about 645 calories per sandwich, Croque Madame 745 calories.

Potatoes O'Brien

Easy

This colorful version of fried potatoes adds bell peppers and chives along with the usual onions to make a side dish with both eye appeal and great taste. Adding the salt at the last minute helps the potatoes crisp without drawing the moisture out of them.

INGREDIENTS

2 teaspoons olive oil

2 teaspoons butter

¼ cup finely diced onions

2 medium red skin potatoes, diced (about 2 cups)

2 tablespoons finely diced bell pepper

2–4 teaspoons chopped chives

Fresh ground sea salt and black pepper

DIRECTIONS

1. Heat the olive oil, butter, and onions in a medium cast-iron frying pan until the butter melts.

2. Add the potatoes, cover, and cook over medium high heat for 5 minutes. Uncover, turn the potatoes around using a spatula, and sprinkle the peppers over the top.

3. Cover and cook another 5 minutes. Uncover, stir around, and season with the chives and black pepper. Continue frying, uncovered, another 3–4 minutes, until the vegetables are browned and cooked to your liking.

4. Season with a few grinds of salt and serve.

Each serving equals approximately 190 calories.

Hazelnut Mocha Lattes

Easy

You can prepare this latte to enjoy either hot or iced. If it's going to be iced, prepare the coffee enough in advance so that it has time to cool down before constructing your latte. Because most chocolate milk now comes made with skim milk, you may wish to finish your drink with a little dollop of sweetened whipped cream for added richness and flavor. Of course, you may wish to add whipped cream to the iced latte, as well; after all, you're celebrating, right?

INGREDIENTS

2 cups coffee, preferably hazelnut flavored

1 cup chocolate ice cream or 1 cup chocolate milk

2 tablespoons hazelnut liqueur or hazelnut flavored syrup

Whipped cream, grated chocolate, and/or toasted diced hazelnuts for topping

DIRECTIONS

1. For hot lattes, heat the chocolate milk in a small saucepan until it's warm but not boiling hot. Combine the hot coffee, warm milk, and hazelnut liqueur or syrup and blend until frothy; pour into two mugs and top with whipped cream and/or other desired toppings.

2. For iced lattes, combine the chocolate ice cream, hazelnut liqueur or syrup, and chilled coffee and blend until smooth and creamy. Pour over ice in tall glasses, add desired toppings, and enjoy. A straw for sipping might be in order here!

Hot latte before toppings is about 120 calories each; iced latte before toppings is about 200 calories each, depending on the brand of ice cream.

GAME DAY GET-TOGETHER

The chili and cheese dip recipes are super easy to prepare, and can be made in advance and heated up just before the Big Game (or during halftime). The brownies or bars and the cornbread may also be made a day in advance, cooled, and stored tightly covered to keep them fresh. The fries are not difficult, but will need someone to keep an eye on them, so plan the timing accordingly. Perhaps they could be prepared in advance as well . . . I've never been able to resist them long enough to find out!

Chili with Beef and Beans
Sweet Potato Oven Fries
(Veggie Platter and Chips with Dip)
(Crusty Bread, Tortilla Chips) or Honey Cornbread (p. 51)
Cocoa Fudge Brownies and/or Peanut Butterscotch Bars (p. 215 and 221)
Beverages of Choice

Chili with Beef and Beans

Easy

This is one of the easiest chili recipes you'll ever concoct, and it's easy to turn it into your signature dish depending on the type of salsa you use. Hot, mild, or somewhere in between; you get to decide! Try serving over your preferred bread or chips, topped with Sweet Potato Oven Fries (p. 269), Jalapeño Cheese Sauce, and condiments of choice for a big platter of tasty goodness. This makes enough for seconds or leftovers.

INGREDIENTS

8–10 ounces 85% ground beef

15-ounce can small red beans

16 ounce jar salsa

2–3 teaspoons chili powder

½ teaspoon garlic salt

Hot sauce to taste

1 cup water

Jalapeño Cheese Sauce

Condiments such as diced onion, avocado, sour cream, shredded cheese

DIRECTIONS

1. Brown the ground beef in a large heavy skillet, breaking it into small pieces. Stir in everything except the cheese sauce and condiments; allow it to simmer, stirring occasionally, about half an hour to blend flavors. Hint: Use the water to rinse out the salsa and bean containers, thereby getting every bit into the chili.

2. Serve with desired condiments, Jalapeño Cheese Sauce, and Sweet Potato Oven Fries if you wish.

This makes 3-4 hearty servings; about 1080 calories total for the chili before adding sauce, toppings, or fries; 360 for 3 servings or 270 for 4 servings.

(continued)

Jalapeño Cheese Sauce

1 tablespoon butter

1 tablespoon flour

⅛ teaspoon salt

⅛ teaspoon paprika

¾ cup milk

1 cup shredded cheddar jack cheese

¼ cup drained pickled jalapeños

DIRECTIONS

1. Melt the butter in a small saucepan over medium heat. Stir in the flour, salt, and paprika.

2. Whisk in the milk all at once and bring to a boil, allowing it to cook for a minute or two to thicken. Stir in the cheese until it's completely melted, being careful not to let the mixture boil at this point.

3. Remove from the heat, stir in the jalapeños, pour into a small dish, and serve. If the sauce cools down too much or gets too thick, simply reheat it over low heat on the stove or microwave it for a few seconds, stirring as needed.

There are about 550 calories total in each batch; gauge individual servings accordingly.

Sweet Potato Oven Fries
Easy-Moderate

Check your sweet potato weight when purchasing them; a single large sweet potato may be enough! Double the batch if you want extras; these crispy little fries are hard to resist!

INGREDIENTS

10–12 ounces sweet potatoes

¼ teaspoon salt

1 teaspoon sugar

Small pinch cayenne pepper

2 tablespoons oil

DIRECTIONS

1. Preheat oven to 425°F. Peel the sweet potato(es) and cut into long thin strips, making them as uniform as possible and trimming off any tapered ends; they will tend to burn otherwise. Immerse in a bowl of cold water for about 5 minutes; this helps remove excess starch, making the fries crisp up easier.

2. Combine the salt, sugar, and cayenne in a small dish; set aside.

3. Drain the sweet potatoes and pat dry with paper towels. Place the sweet potatoes on a baking sheet that has been lightly oiled or sprayed with non-stick spray. Drizzle the oil evenly over the potatoes, tossing them to coat well.

4. Bake in oven until crispy and brown, turning occasionally, for about 35–45 minutes. This time may vary from oven to oven; start keeping fairly close tabs on them after about 30 minutes. Somewhere along the way, the fries will morph from simply being very soft to a point where they begin to brown and caramelize a little on the edges; you'll want to remove them before they actually start to burn.

5. Sprinkle the hot fries with the sugar salt mixture, tossing gently to coat well. Serve hot with chili and cheese sauce, or just enjoy them as is.

There are about 250 calories in one serving of these fries, 500 calories for the whole batch.

HARVEST FEAST

Thanksgiving dinner is the quintessential family meal, but if your family is small, you may not wish to tackle an entire turkey. In that case, Cornish game hen will fly to your rescue! This menu has some of the more complex recipes in this book and they're worth every extra minute you may spend. As with the other special meals, you can get lots of the cooking out of the way in advance; the cheesecake will be better if prepared a day or two ahead, and the sweet potatoes can be wrapped in foil and refrigerated before the final baking step. Set the roll dough to rise before preparing the Cornish hen. Once the hen has been popped in the oven you'll have almost two hours to prepare the green beans and finish baking the rolls and sweet potatoes.

Roast Cornish Hen with Cranberry-Orange Stuffing and Glaze
Coconut Pecan Twice-Baked Sweet Potatoes
Green Beans and Mushrooms with Crispy Shallots
Crescent Rolls (p. 57)
Pumpkin Apricot Cheesecake

Roast Cornish Hen with Cranberry-Orange Stuffing and Glaze

Complex

Why not try roasted Cornish hen for your next Thanksgiving feast? This little bird is sized just right for two people, and is certainly easier and more economical to prepare than a full-fledged turkey! It also looks quite glorious, coming to the table enrobed in a colorful and flavorful glaze.

INGREDIENTS

4 tablespoons smooth cranberry sauce (canned or homemade)

4 tablespoons orange juice

1 tablespoon honey

3 tablespoons butter, divided

2 tablespoons minced shallots

2 tablespoons chopped pecans

2 tablespoons diced dates

2 thin slices whole-grain bread, toasted, to equal 1 cup loosely packed torn bread

1 teaspoon minced fresh rosemary or ½ teaspoon crumbled dried

1 Cornish game hen, about 2 pounds total

Salt and pepper

¾ cup chicken broth

¼ cup white wine or additional chicken broth

1 tablespoon flour

DIRECTIONS

1. Preheat oven to 350°F. Prepare the glaze by heating the cranberry sauce, orange juice, honey, and 1 tablespoon of the butter in a small saucepan and bringing to a boil. Remove from the heat and set aside.

2. Melt another tablespoon of the butter in a small skillet or saucepan and lightly sauté the shallots until softened but not browned. Add in the pecans, dates, torn bread, rosemary, and 5 tablespoons of the cranberry orange sauce. Spoon the stuffing into the game hen, firming in the end as needed.

3. Melt the remaining 1 tablespoon of butter in a small roasting pan. Sprinkle with freshly ground salt and pepper and place the hen, breast side down, into the pan. Roast for approximately one half hour. Turn the hen breast side up and roast for another 45–60 minutes, basting twice with the remaining cranberry orange sauce, until juices run clear when a fork or sharp knife tip is inserted near the thigh.

4. Once roasting is complete, remove from the oven, place on a warm serving plate, and set it aside to rest for up to half an hour, while baking the rolls, finishing vegetables, and making the gravy.

5. For the gravy, combine the broth, white wine, and flour, stirring into the pan juices until smooth. Either heat in the pan if it's stovetop safe or pour into a small saucepan. Bring the mixture to boiling, whisking frequently, until the gravy thickens. Pour the gravy into a small gravy boat or pitcher, straining through a sieve first if you wish. Split the hen down the center to serve.

According to the label, 4 ounces of Cornish game hen provides you with 220 calories. Since so much of the little birds consist of bones, I'll leave it to you to "guesstimate" the calories you might consume in a half . . . I don't think it would be many more than the 4-ounce listing. The stuffing in this recipe will give you 115 calories per serving, the gravy as prepared 35 per ¼ cup.

Coconut Pecan Twice-Baked Sweet Potatoes
Moderate

Coconut and pecans complement the almost candy-like flavor of the baked sweet potatoes in this recipe. If you really love coconut, try adding coconut milk instead of half-and-half; you can always use up the rest of the can making Sweet Coconut French Toast (p. 26), Coconut Chicken Soup (p. 63), or Chicken Satay with Coconut Rice (p. 130). Conversely, if you prefer not to add coconut and/or pecans to the filling, the potatoes will still be delicious without them.

INGREDIENTS

10–12 ounces sweet potato (1 large or 2 small)

2 tablespoons brown sugar

2 teaspoons butter

2 tablespoons light coconut milk or half-and-half

¼ teaspoon vanilla extract

⅛ teaspoon cinnamon

Pinch of nutmeg

Pinch of salt

2 tablespoons flaked coconut

2 tablespoons finely chopped pecans

DIRECTIONS

1. Microwave the potatoes until soft; time will vary, depending on the microwave and size of potatoes. For smaller sweet potatoes I plan on about 8 minutes plus some resting time to finish the cooking process. If need be, you may bake them instead; about 45 minutes at 350°F would be about right for 5–6 ounce potatoes. Again, allow them to rest for about 15 minutes or up to an hour.

2. Cut the large potato in half horizontally, or slice a thin strip from the tops of the smaller potatoes. Carefully scoop out as much of the flesh as you can, leaving a very thin shell inside the skin; place on a small baking sheet.

3. Mash the sweet potato flesh, adding in the brown sugar, butter, coconut milk or half-and-half, vanilla, and seasonings. Once it's nice and smooth, stir in the coconut and pecans. Mound the mixture back into the potato skins.

4. At this point, you may either twice-bake the potatoes right away or lightly cover with plastic wrap or foil and refrigerate for up to 3 days. The oven temperature can vary between 375–425°F for the heating process; higher works better for the still warm freshly stuffed potatoes, which should heat for about 15 minutes. Chilled potatoes will probably take about ½–¾ of an hour, depending on how many are being prepared at once; unwrap and place on a baking tray.

Each twice-baked sweet potato or potato half is about 285 calories.

Green Beans and Mushrooms with Crispy Shallots
Moderate

Here is a mini variation on a classic holiday side dish. Shallots add unique crunch and flavor. Try varying the mushrooms used according to individual preference. This dish will make two generous servings.

INGREDIENTS

6 ounces fresh green beans, trimmed (about 1½ cups)

2 tablespoons butter, divided

1 shallot, peeled and thinly sliced (about ¼ cup)

1 cup sliced mushrooms

1 teaspoon cornstarch

¼ teaspoon salt

½ teaspoon Worcestershire sauce

¼ cup milk

¼ teaspoon dill weed

¼ cup sour cream

DIRECTIONS

1. Place the green beans in salted water to cover and boil for about 15 minutes, until just tender but still bright green. In a small heavy skillet, heat 1 tablespoon of the butter and sauté the shallots until they are crispy and brown. Remove from the pan and set aside.

2. Add the remaining butter to the pan along with the mushrooms and sauté for about 5 minutes, until the mushrooms are softened and slightly browned. Stir in the cornstarch, salt, and Worcestershire sauce. Add the milk and cook just until thickened and bubbly. Stir in the dill and sour cream.

3. Place the drained green beans in a serving bowl. Spoon the mushroom sauce over the beans. Top with the fried shallots just before serving.

The casserole contains about 330 calories, or approximately 165 per generous serving.

Pumpkin Apricot Cheesecake

Complex

If you like a little pumpkin for your Thanksgiving meal but not too much, this cheesecake may just fill the bill. Rather than relying on a lot of spice, Pumpkin Apricot Cheesecake is enhanced with almond, apricot, and just a hint of orange. (Extra pumpkin can be used up in Pumpkin Pancakes (p. 19) or Curried Pumpkin Apple Soup (p. 280). Try piping the whipped cream topping through an inexpensive pastry bag for an extra festive appearance. This will yield 4 generous servings so you can enjoy leftovers. You may either use a small spring-form pan or a 6" round cake tin; directions for this are included in the recipe.

INGREDIENTS

¼ cup slivered almonds

¼ cup dried apricots (6 whole)

¼ cup water

¼ cup orange juice

2" cinnamon stick or ¼ teaspoon ground cinnamon

2 individual packets snack-sized shortbread cookies or 6 full-sized shortbread cookies

1 tablespoon butter

½ teaspoon almond extract, divided

8 ounces cream cheese or light cream cheese

½ cup plus 2 tablespoons confectioner's sugar, divided

⅛ teaspoon nutmeg

6 tablespoons pumpkin purée

1 egg

6 tablespoons heavy cream

DIRECTIONS

1. I like using my 6" round cake pan for this recipe. Line it with enough foil to hang over the edges, pressing firmly around the inner side of the pan. Butter the foil and set aside.

2. Lightly toast the almonds at 325°F for about 5 minutes, until they are light golden brown; don't overbrown them.

3. Meanwhile, combine the apricots, water, orange juice, and cinnamon in a small saucepan. Bring to a boil, reduce heat to low, and simmer for 8–10 minutes, until all but about 1 tablespoon of the cooking liquid is absorbed. Remove from the heat and allow the apricots to cool slightly before removing and finely dicing three of them.

4. Remove the other apricots and the cinnamon stick if you used one, cutting each apricot in half. You can either discard the cinnamon stick or "recycle" it in some hot

(continued)

mulled cider. Cover the halved apricots and refrigerate until ready to use. Combine the diced apricots with the remaining cooking liquid in the cooking pan and set aside.

5. Combine the shortbread cookies and 2 tablespoons of the toasted almonds in a blender or food processor and whirl until they have formed fine crumbs. Melt the butter and combine with ¼ teaspoon of the almond extract. Stir in the crumb mixture until well blended. Pat lightly into the prepared pan and set aside.

6. Place the softened cream cheese in a small mixing bowl and whip until smooth. Add in the diced apricots and cooking liquid, ½ cup of the confectioner's sugar, and the nutmeg, beating until light and fluffy. On low speed, beat in the pumpkin purée and then the egg, scraping the bowl as needed.

7. Pour evenly over the prepared crust and bake at 325°F for 45–50 minutes, until the top is firm to gentle touch. Cool in the pan to room temperature and then refrigerate at least 2 hours; overnight is even better. If you're using a cake pan, carefully invert the pan, tipping the cheesecake out onto the palm of your hand. Peel off the foil and gently place the cheesecake right side up on a serving plate.

8. Before serving, whip the cream with the remaining 2 tablespoons of confectioner's sugar. Pipe the whipped cream decoratively over the cheesecake; add the reserved apricot halves and serve.

There are about 2160 calories total when made with regular cream cheese; 540 per ¼ serving of cheesecake.

CHRISTMAS DINNER

Ah, Christmas, when we're all of good cheer! You'll cheer for this Christmas mini-feast as well. Pork tenderloin is the star of our Christmas dinner, preceded by a smooth and sweet curried soup. After enjoying the pork with accompaniments of mashed potatoes, colorful jellied salad, green vegetable of choice, and homemade rolls, finish the feast with Italian inspired semi freddo and homemade cookies. The soup, salad, semi freddo, and cookies can all be made a day or two in advance, leaving just the roast, vegetables, and rolls for the actual day. Although Christmas only comes once a year, you may just want to enjoy this meal over and over again.

Curried Pumpkin and Apple Soup
Ginger Honey Pork Roast with Glazed Onions
Creamy Mashed Potatoes (p. 165)
(Green Vegetable of Choice)
Crimson and White Jellied Salad
Honey Oatmeal Pan Rolls or Crescent Rolls (p. 55 and 57)
Spumoni Semi Freddo
Assorted Cookies (p. 207–211)

Curried Pumpkin Apple Soup

Easy

Although this soup is a snap to put together, you may also prepare it up to 3 days in advance; store, covered, in the refrigerator and either warm it gently or serve chilled.

INGREDIENTS

1½ cups vegetable broth

1 cup unsweetened applesauce

1 cup puréed pumpkin

½ teaspoon curry powder

2 tablespoons pure maple syrup

DIRECTIONS

1. Combine everything in a small saucepan. Bring to a boil, stirring to blend well. Reduce heat slightly and simmer for about 5 minutes.

2. Serve your soup either hot, at room temperature, or chilled, garnished with a few slices of apple if you wish.

Each serving is about 150 calories. This recipe is 300 calories in its entirety.

Ginger Honey Pork Roast with Glazed Onions
Easy-Moderate

Some more recent recipe sources cook certain cuts of pork so that they are still rare when served. Because I grew up in a time when pork was always served well done (as a preventative against the pork-borne illness trichinosis) I have retained my liking for fully cooked pork. Not only will your tenderloin remain tender when roasted according to this recipe, it will also develop a lovely glaze in the process.

INGREDIENTS

2 tablespoons honey

2 tablespoons butter

1 tablespoon soy sauce

1 teaspoon grated ginger root

1½ cups frozen pearl onions

12-ounce pork tenderloin

DIRECTIONS

1. Preheat oven to 400°F. Combine the honey, butter, soy sauce, and grated ginger in a small saucepan and heat gently, stirring, until the butter melts. Remove from the heat.

2. Place the pearl onions in a large measuring cup or small bowl and pour on hot tap water to thaw but not cook them. Drain well and combine with 2 tablespoons of the glaze.

3. Butter or spray with non-stick cooking spray a small roasting pan or 9" cake pan. Place the pork in the middle and add the onions evenly around it. Drizzle 2 tablespoons of the glaze over the pork, spreading to coat well. Add in ¼ cup water and place in the preheated oven. Roast for approximately 1 hour, stirring the onions and pouring the rest of the glaze over the pork after about half an hour.

4. During the last 15 minutes, stir the onions and juices in the pan fairly frequently, re-glazing the pork each time you do. Although this recipe practically cooks itself, the last 5–10 minutes are a little tricky; you want the pan juices to reduce to a syrupy consistency; too much and they will burn, too little and you won't have your nice flavorful glaze. When done, the pork should be glazed amber brown, as should the onions. Remove from oven and allow to rest while you put the finishing touches on the rest of the meal.

Contains about 730 calories total; 365 per serving.

Crimson and White Jellied Salad

Complex

Although this jellied salad takes a little extra work, it is so very worth it. Made-from-scratch red raspberry jell glows in the top layer, covering a snowy white base studded with mini marshmallows, bits of pineapple, and crimson raspberries. And, it's as delicious to eat as it is beautiful to behold.

INGREDIENTS

1½ cups fresh or frozen unsweetened raspberries, divided

1 packet unsweetened gelatin powder, divided

7 tablespoons sugar, divided

1 (4-ounce) individual serving pineapple tidbits in juice or ½ of an 8-ounce can

½ cup mini marshmallows

¼ cup juice, drained from the pineapple

1 tablespoon lemon juice

1 ounce cream cheese

2 tablespoons sour cream

DIRECTIONS

1. Combine 1 cup of the raspberries and ½ cup water in a small saucepan. Bring to a boil, reduce heat, and simmer for about 5 minutes. Remove from heat and allow the mixture to stand for about ½ hour, until it has cooled to room temperature. Pour into a fine sieve and allow it to drain, undisturbed, for another ½ hour. For clear, beautiful gelatin, it's important that you don't try to force any of the raspberry mixture through the sieve; just let it drip naturally.

2. When this process is over, you should have about ¼ cup of ruby red clear raspberry juice. If you have a bit more, use some in place of the water in the next step; if you don't have quite enough, add water to the juice to equal ¼ cup.

3. Sprinkle ½ teaspoon of the gelatin over the cooled raspberry juice to soften while you bring ¼ cup of water to boiling in a small saucepan. Stir in the raspberry juice mixture and 2 tablespoons of the sugar until the gelatin and sugar are totally dissolved. Pour gently into a 2½ cup jelly mold or bowl that has been lightly oiled or spritzed with non-stick cooking spray. Refrigerate until set; about 30–45 minutes.

4. Meanwhile, drain the pineapple, reserving the juice; combine the tidbits with the mini marshmallows and refrigerate. If necessary, add water to the pineapple juice to equal ¼ cup.

(continued)

5. Sprinkle the remaining gelatin (2 teaspoons) over the pineapple juice and set aside to soften. Heat ½ cup water to boiling in a small saucepan; stir in the pineapple juice mixture, lemon juice, and 5 tablespoons of sugar until the gelatin and sugar are thoroughly dissolved. Add in ½ cup of cold water; set aside.

6. In a small mixing bowl, beat the cream cheese and sour cream together until smooth and creamy. Slowly add the gelatin mixture, starting with a very little at a time, beating smooth after each addition. Once it has all been integrated, chill the mixture until it mounds (semi-set but still able to stir).

7. Fold in the pineapple and mini marshmallows, and last, the remaining raspberries (if you're using frozen, keep them frozen through this step). Pour over the raspberry layer and continue to chill until totally set; at least 2 hours or better yet overnight. Remember, longer chilling time won't hurt jellied salads, but too little chilling time will.

8. When you're ready to serve, dip the jelly mold or bowl briefly in hot water and turn out onto a serving plate.

Total calories are about 715; 180 calories in ¼ of the salad.

Spumoni Semi Freddo

Moderate-Complex

This multi-layered frozen dessert is concocted from a rich mousse-like custard base, flavored three ways. "Semi freddo" means semi frozen in Italian, and refers to the manner in which it's frozen—by pouring into a pan rather than churning it in an ice cream maker. Use either a 4"x 6" three cup Pyrex pan or 6" round, deep cake pan, lining the pan of choice with overlapping plastic wrap or pieces of baking parchment paper cut to shape. Make sure there's some overlap to cover the entire pan up over the edges, as the custard mousse will mostly fill it up. When thoroughly frozen, the semi freddo is inverted and removed from the pan; the wrap or paper, which enable the semi freddo to slide right out, are peeled away at the same time. If the edges seem wrinkled or uneven, they can be smoothed with a flat knife dipped in hot water. Cutting is also made easier by using a sharp knife dipped in hot water or held under a faucet of running hot water. Although somewhat time-consuming to construct due to the freezing time, it may easily be made up to a week in advance, unmolding just before serving time. Store leftovers, covered, in the freezer for a week or two longer. Warm Mocha Orange Sauce is delicious drizzled over the top just before serving.

INGREDIENTS

2 eggs

½ cup sugar

½ cup milk

¾ teaspoon almond extract

⅛ teaspoon powdered cardamom

2 tablespoons finely chopped pistachios

2 drops each red and green food coloring

⅛ teaspoon orange extract or ¼ teaspoon
   grated orange zest

⅛ teaspoon cherry extract, optional

6 maraschino cherries, well drained and
   finely diced

¼ teaspoon vanilla extract

1 ounce grated semi-sweet chocolate or
   2 tablespoons toasted coconut or both

¾ cup heavy cream, divided

DIRECTIONS

1. Beat the eggs with the sugar until they are thick and ivory colored. Meanwhile, heat the milk in a small saucepan until just under boiling. Beat into the sugar and egg mixture, return to the saucepan and cook, stirring constantly, until a candy thermometer* registers 165–170°F; this is the safe temperature for eggs to destroy possible salmonella contamination.

2. Remove from the heat and stir in the almond extract. Measure out ¾ cup of the mixture into each of two small bowls. Into one bowl add the cardamom, chopped

(continued)

pistachios, and two drops of green food coloring. To the second bowl add the orange extract or rind, cherry flavoring, diced cherries, and 2 drops of red food coloring. Pour the remaining custard base into a third small bowl and stir in the vanilla, grated chocolate, and/or toasted coconut. Chill all 3 bowls of custard base until they are very cold.

3. Whip ¼ cup of the cream to soft peaks; fold into the cherry mixture and immediately turn into prepared pan. Freeze for approximately 1 hour, until the mixture is partially frozen. Whip another ¼ cup of the cream and fold into the vanilla almond mixture; carefully pour over the cherry layer. Freeze for another hour. Repeat with the remaining ¼ cup of cream and pistachio mixture.

4. Freeze everything until it's thoroughly frozen; at least 4 hours depending on the efficiency of your freezer, although overnight is better. When you're ready to serve, turn it out onto a serving plate, remove the plastic wrap or parchment paper, and smooth the surface with a flat knife dipped in hot water, if necessary. Slicing is also easier using a sharp knife dipped in hot water or held under the faucet.

The total calories for Spumoni Semi Freddo when made with both the toasted coconut and grated chocolate are about 1480, or 370 per ¼ serving.

* For the safest preparation you should plan to use a candy thermometer to determine the temperature of the cooking eggs; too hot and they'll boil and curdle, too cool and possible food contaminants won't be killed. Once upon a time the gauge for determining if a custard was sufficiently cooked was to allow some to run from a metal spoon; if it coated the spoon, it was considered done.

(continued)

Warm Mocha Orange Sauce

INGREDIENTS

3 tablespoons coffee

3 tablespoons heavy cream

3 tablespoons light corn syrup

3 ounces semi-sweet chocolate, chopped

½ teaspoon pure orange extract or grated
 orange zest

DIRECTIONS

1. Combine the coffee, cream, and corn syrup in a small saucepan. Bring just to boiling; remove from heat and stir in the chocolate until it's completely melted.

2. Stir in the orange extract or zest and serve warm over the semi freddo. This sauce is also easily re-heated either on the stovetop or in the microwave; just be careful it doesn't burn. Leftover sauce should be stored, covered, in the refrigerator.

This makes just over ½ cup; 750 calories total or about 190 per ¼ serving (2 tablespoons).

CONVERSION CHARTS

(These conversions are rounded for convenience)

Ingredient	Cups/Tablespoons/ Teaspoons	Ounces	Grams/Milliliters
Butter	1 cup/ 16 tablespoons/ 2 sticks	8 ounces	230 grams
Cheese, shredded	1 cup	4 ounces	110 grams
Cream cheese	1 tablespoon	0.5 ounce	14.5 grams
Cornstarch	1 tablespoon	0.3 ounce	8 grams
Flour, all-purpose	1 cup/1 tablespoon	4.5 ounces/0.3 ounce	125 grams/8 grams
Flour, whole wheat	1 cup	4 ounces	120 grams
Fruit, dried	1 cup	4 ounces	120 grams
Fruits or veggies, chopped	1 cup	5 to 7 ounces	145 to 200 grams
Fruits or veggies, pureed	1 cup	8.5 ounces	245 grams
Honey, maple syrup, or corn syrup	1 tablespoon	0.75 ounce	20 grams
Liquids: cream, milk, water, or juice	1 cup	8 fluid ounces	240 milliliters
Oats	1 cup	5.5 ounces	150 grams
Salt	1 teaspoon	0.2 ounce	6 grams
Spices: cinnamon, cloves, ginger, or nutmeg (ground)	1 teaspoon	0.2 ounce	5 milliliters
Sugar, brown, firmly packed	1 cup	7 ounces	200 grams
Sugar, white	1 cup/1 tablespoon	7 ounces/0.5 ounce	200 grams/12.5 grams
Vanilla extract	1 teaspoon	0.2 ounce	4 grams

OVEN TEMPERATURES

Fahrenheit	Celsius	Gas Mark
225°	110°	¼
250°	120°	½
275°	140°	1
300°	150°	2
325°	160°	3
350°	180°	4
375°	190°	5
400°	200°	6
425°	220°	7
450°	230°	8

INDEX